Harvey J. Hodges.
Feb. 7th 1936.

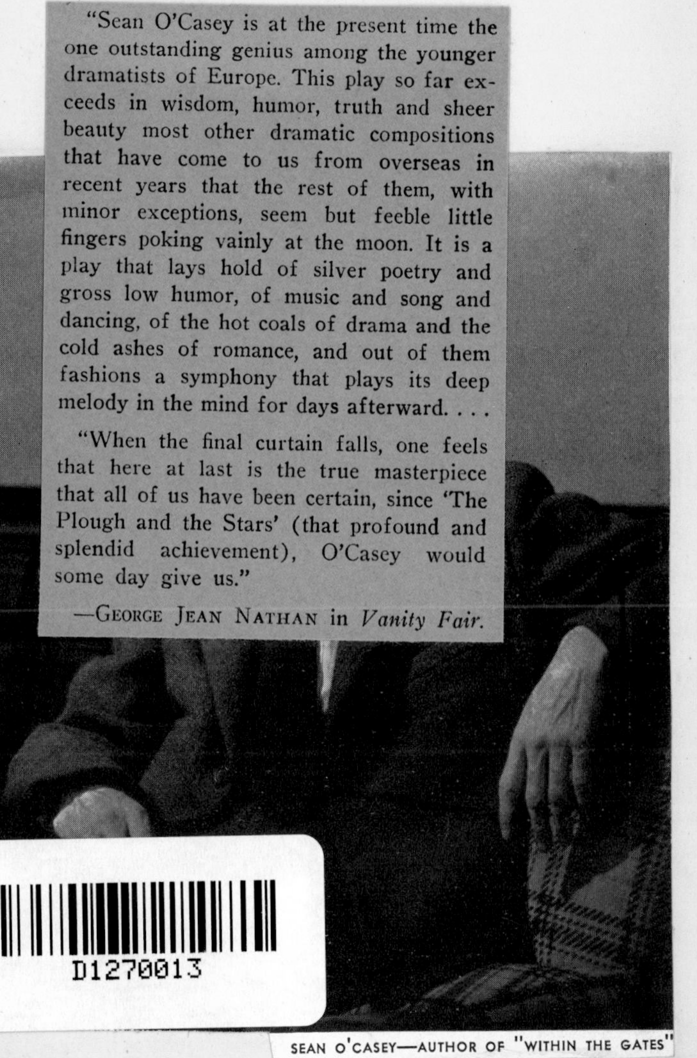

"Sean O'Casey is at the present time the one outstanding genius among the younger dramatists of Europe. This play so far exceeds in wisdom, humor, truth and sheer beauty most other dramatic compositions that have come to us from overseas in recent years that the rest of them, with minor exceptions, seem but feeble little fingers poking vainly at the moon. It is a play that lays hold of silver poetry and gross low humor, of music and song and dancing, of the hot coals of drama and the cold ashes of romance, and out of them fashions a symphony that plays its deep melody in the mind for days afterward. . . .

"When the final curtain falls, one feels that here at last is the true masterpiece that all of us have been certain, since 'The Plough and the Stars' (that profound and splendid achievement), O'Casey would some day give us."

—George Jean Nathan in *Vanity Fair.*

SEAN O'CASEY—AUTHOR OF "WITHIN THE GATES"

WITHIN THE GATES

THE MACMILLAN COMPANY
NEW YORK · BOSTON · CHICAGO · DALLAS
ATLANTA · SAN FRANCISCO

MACMILLAN & CO., LIMITED
LONDON · BOMBAY · CALCUTTA
MELBOURNE

THE MACMILLAN COMPANY
OF CANADA, LIMITED
TORONTO

WITHIN THE GATES

A PLAY OF FOUR SCENES IN A LONDON PARK

BY

SEAN O'CASEY

NEW YORK
THE MACMILLAN COMPANY
1935

Published, January, 1934.
Reprinted, May, November (twice), 1934;
January, 1935.

PRINTED IN THE UNITED STATES OF AMERICA
BY THE POLYGRAPHIC COMPANY OF AMERICA, N.Y.

Notes for Production

THE Proscenium borders and trimmings should be removed so as to allow the trees to rise as high as possible, and, generally, to improve the aspect of spaciousness.

The scenic effects should be as simple as possible, suggesting, rather than emphasising, the features of the Park; and colours should be the prime way of indicating the different seasons.

From the BISHOP'S "Benedicti vos a Domino", in the Fourth Act, to the departure of the DOWN-AND-OUTS, the dialogue should, if possible, be intoned.

If possible, the Curtain intervening between the opening of the play and the scenes following, should be one showing the Park Gates, stiff and formal, dignified and insolent. The bars should shine with the silver gleam of aluminium paint, and cross or diagonal bars should be a deep and sombre black. All space between the bars should be dark—but not too dark—green. The gates proper are flanked by generous panels of a vivid yellow, representing the piers, lower than the bars, and topped by copings of orange-coloured panels. This curtain, when it is pulled back, represents the opening of the gates; and, when it falls back into its place, represents the closing of the gates: or, the outline of the gates may be suggested on the curtain.

The above idea of a front curtain was derived from Eugene O'Neill's suggestion of a front curtain for his great play, *Mourning Becomes Electra*.

CHARACTERS

(In the order of their first appearance)

THE DREAMER.
THE BISHOP.
THE BISHOP'S SISTER.
1ST CHAIR ATTENDANT.
2ND CHAIR ATTENDANT.
A BOY.
THE ATHEIST.
THE POLICEWOMAN.
THE YOUNG MAN IN PLUS-FOURS.
THE SCARLET WOMAN.
1ST NURSEMAID.
2ND NURSEMAID.
A GUARDSMAN.
THE GARDENER.
1ST EVANGELIST.
2ND EVANGELIST.
THE YOUNG WHORE.
A YOUNG SALVATION ARMY OFFICER.
THE FOREMAN.
THE OLD WOMAN.
THE MAN IN THE BOWLER HAT.
THE MAN WITH THE STICK.
THE MAN IN THE TRILBY HAT.
1ST PLATFORM SPEAKER.
2ND PLATFORM SPEAKER.
A YOUNG MAN.
THE MAN IN THE BURBERRY.
A GROUP OF DOWN-AND-OUTS.

A Chorus of Young Men and Girls.
Birds.

SCENE I

Within a Park.
On a Spring Morning.

SCENE II

Within a Park.
On a Summer Noon.

SCENE III

Within a Park.
On an Autumn Evening.

SCENE IV

Within a Park.
On a Winter's Night.

SCENE I

Spring. Morning.

Within the Park on a Spring morning.

A clear, cold, blue sky, against which is shown, in places, the interlaced, dark-brown branches of trees, dotted with green, yellow, and red buds.

The green sward in front slopes up towards the back, but in no way high enough to prevent a view of the spaciousness of the Park behind. In the centre of the slope are a few wide steps leading to the top, where, a little to one side, stands a War Memorial in the form of a steel-helmeted soldier, the head bent on the breast, skeleton-like hands leaning on the butt-end of a rifle.

Bushes allow the figure to be seen only from the waist up. The body and arms of the figure are shaped in a sharply defined way; the hat a wide circle, and the features are cut in long, sharp, and angular lines. The figure stands out grey against the blue sky and the green shrubs, and seems to be shrinking back from the growing interests brought into being by new life and other interests.

The rise of the slope is sprinkled with large, formalised figures of daffodils.

At the foot of the slope are paths branching to the right and to the left, that on the left flowing into a wider one encircling the Park lake, from which can be occasionally heard the cries of the water-fowl swimming on the water, or preening themselves on the banks.

Birds are heard singing in a subdued but busy way, as they search for food, or build their nests.

Formally shaped chairs are here and there, and one or two stiff and dignified-looking benches are near the foot of the slope. They are painted so as to mingle with the colours of the scene, and are hardly noticeable. The scheme of colour is a delicate green and light blue, patterned by the yellow daffodils and the bare, bud-dotted branches of the trees.

As the gates are opening, the DREAMER *enters, and passes through them into the Park. He is gazing with an intensely dreaming expression at a paper which he holds in his left hand. His right hand, holding a short pencil, moves in a gentle, dreamy way, beating time, as he murmurs the opening bars of "Our Mother, the Earth, is a maiden again". He crosses out as the* CHORUS *enters, singing, followed by various people, who move about at the back, up, down, and about the paths, without jostle or confusion.*

A CHORUS *of young girls and boys, representing trees and flowers, enter, singing.*

First a girl, whose skirt represents a white crocus, veined with blue; next a boy in black on whose breast is a stylised pattern of a beech tree leaf; then a girl whose skirt represents a blue cornflower; next a boy on whose breast is a formally shaped oak leaf; then a girl whose skirt represents a daffodil; next a boy on whose breast is the pattern of a maple leaf.

The CHORUS *remain in front, while the* CROWD *move about as they listen, or when they join in the singing.*

CHORUS (*singing*):

Our mother, the earth, is a maiden again, young, fair, and a maiden again.

CHORUS:

Our mother, the earth, is a maiden again, young, fair, and a maiden again.

Her thoughts are a dance as she seeks out her Bridegroom, the Sun, through the lovely

confusion of singing of birds, and of blossom and bud.
She feels the touch of his hand on her hair, on her cheeks, in the budding of trees,
She feels the warm kiss of his love on her mouth, on her breast, as she dances along

CROWD (*joining in*):

Through the lovely confusion of singing of birds and of blossom and bud.
Her thoughts are a dance as she seeks out her Bridegroom, the Sun, through the lovely confusion of singing of birds, and of blossom and bud.

CHORUS:

She hears the fiercely sung song of the birds, busy building new homes in the hedge;
She hears a challenge to life and to death as she dances along

CROWD (*joining in*):

Through the lovely confusion of singing of birds and of blossom and bud.
Her thoughts are a dance as she seeks out her Bridegroom, the Sun, through the lovely confusion of singing of birds, and of blossom and bud.

CHORUS and CROWD:

Our mother, the earth, is a maiden again, young, fair, and a maiden again;

Our mother, the earth, is a maiden again, she's young, and is fair, and a maiden again!

(*While the last line is being sung, the* CROWD *and the* CHORUS *go out by different ways, leaving only the* BISHOP *and his* SISTER *rambling round.*

The BISHOP *is a heavily built man of sixty or so. His head, his feet, and hands are large; his voice, once deep and sonorous, has become a little husky. The pretentious briskness of his movements are an attempt to hide from others the fact that he is beginning to fail. He is anxious to show to all he meets that he is an up-to-the-present-minute clergyman, and that those who wear the stole are, on the whole, a lusty, natural, broad-minded, cheery crowd. He is in a black cassock, wears a purple stock round his neck, and his head is covered with a black hat shaped like a diminished mitre. A black ribbon is round his neck, and from the ends of this, which meet on his chest, hangs a large red cross, on which is a white figure of the Saviour. In his right hand he carries a large stick, the top of which is shaped like a shepherd's crook.*

His SISTER *is a few years younger, grey-haired, stiff, and formal. She has more common sense than her brother, but, while there is a suggestion of good-nature about the* BISHOP, *there is no suggestion whatever of softness about the form or manner of his* SISTER. *She carries a paper bag in her hand.*)

BISHOP'S SISTER (*grimly*). This fad of getting into closer touch with the common people is absurd, Gilbert; it's ridiculous.

BISHOP (*amiably*). The Church must keep alive, alive o, and up-to-date, dear. Up-to-date. Get amongst the people; get them to talk with us, joke with us, then we may expect them to pray with us.

BISHOP'S SISTER. Oh, let the ordinary clergy do that if they want to; but a bishop—it's absurd!

BISHOP (*changing the subject*). Shall we give these few remaining crumbs to the birds, dear?

(*He wanders down the path on the left, leading to the lakeside, followed by his* SISTER, *and can be heard calling loudly to the birds swimming on the water.*)

VOICE OF BISHOP (*calling to the birds*). Chuck chuck, chuck chuck chuck chuck!

(*The two* PARK CHAIR ATTENDANTS *enter, one from the right, and the other from the left, each carrying a green-painted deck-chair. The one who has entered on the left, crosses to the right; the one who has entered on the right, crosses to the left, and both, at the same time, leave down the chairs in suitable places. One is young and thin, and the other is old and stocky, and both are in the last lap of physical decay. One has a stiff right leg, and the other has a stiff left one. They are dressed in long, khaki-coloured cotton coats, and wear peaked caps.*)

The OLDER ONE. 'Ow's the old leg, 'Erbert?

The YOUNGER ONE (*with a movement indicating hopelessness*). Aw, Gord! 'Ow's yourn?

OLDER ONE (*with a similar movement*). Aw—sime wye, with honours!

(*A pause.*)

YOUNGER ONE. Long hours to go yet before we know fer certain if it's a frisk or a fall.

OLDER ONE (*gloomily*). As the minutes pass me 'opes er getting fyneter en' fyneter.

YOUNGER ONE (*hopefully*). Pedigree's good, enyhow; couldn't 'ave 'ad a better dam or sire.

OLDER ONE (*dubiously*). Doesn't alwyes count, Godfrey, doesn't alwyes count.

YOUNGER ONE (*yearningly*). If 'e only 'as the stamina to stick it to the end of the course, en' win even by a short 'ead—oh, wot it would mean to us!

OLDER ONE. Difference between poverty en' wealth fer a month or more.

(*A pause.*)

YOUNGER ONE. 'Ere, Bysil, you 'olds 'ard to a belief in the power of pryer—do you or don't you?

OLDER ONE (*cautiously*). Sure,—with limitytions, of course.

YOUNGER ONE. Think we might charnce a pryer for a win withaht it being answered in the wrong wye?

BISHOP'S VOICE (*calling the water-fowl*). Chuck chuck, chuck chuck chuck chuck!

OLDER ONE (*with resentful dismay*). Oh, wot did you warnt to go en' mention wot you said in connection with wot we were torking abaht! The cautious wye you said it showed you guessed it was dinegerous. Now there'll be nothing but pryers for the success of wot we were torking abaht apushing their wye into me 'ead en' me gathering thoughts together to push 'em aht agine.

YOUNG ONE (*apologetically*). As 'old the Fort 'as a good jockey up, en' we know 'e 'as, I thought a cautious bit of a pryer fer 'im en' the 'orse might be en ide.

OLDER ONE (*irritably*). Leave me aht of it, leave me aht of it. Don't keep 'inting en' 'inting at it. If you warnt to charnce wot you 'ave in your mind in connection with wot we were torking abaht, git on with it, but don't go 'inting en' 'inting it into my mind!

(*They cross by each other, one indignant, the other apologetic, and go off, one to the right, and the other to the left.*

When they have gone, a BOY *runs in, right, knocks the chairs flat, and then runs out.*

The DREAMER *and the* ATHEIST *appear on the slope above, and come slowly down the path to the front.*

The DREAMER *is a young man, lithely built, thin and pale, but he carries himself buoyantly. His features are rugged; his eyes are bright, sometimes flashing in an imaginative mood, but usually quiet and dreamy-looking. His head is covered with a soft black, broad-brimmed hat, and he is wearing a tightly belted trench mackintosh. Outside the trench coat, around his neck is a light, vivid orange scarf.*

The ATHEIST *is a lean, wiry man of fifty.*

His face is thin and very gaunt-looking, with bushy grey eyebrows, and thin lips tightly closed, that move nervously when circumstances do not permit him to answer immediately a statement with which he disagrees. He is wearing a well-worn tweed top-coat which looks to be too tight for him, a soft, faded grey trilby hat, and a black muffler round his neck.

Both of them look thoughtful as they come down the path.)

ATHEIST. She's pretty, damn pretty, Dreamer, en' 'as a mind, a swift intelligence of 'er own; but she's 'ot stuff, there's no daht abaht it. Glad she ain't my kid.

DREAMER. She's a lovely kid, I think. Try her out once more, man; give her another chance.

ATHEIST. 'Be useless. Besides, I've no intention of going back to a regular life—doesn't suit me.

DREAMER. Who was the real daddy of this remarkable young lady?

ATHEIST. Stoodent studying theology, the story goes. The mother, when she knew wot was 'appening, knocked at the College gites, but she was 'unted awye. 'Is people sent 'er some money—think they send 'er some still. When the kid was a few years in the world, the mother 'anded 'er over to the nuns, who, when they heard the news, put 'er in a special prison of piety en' pryer. Would you believe it, Dreamer, when the kid was 'aving 'er bath, she 'ad to wash 'erself under a gown!

DREAMER. My God, turning the song of life into a mea maxima culpa!

ATHEIST (*bitterly*). En' aht of this close-the-eyes-en'-keep-it-dark gime, the girl 'as got a wild desire to show 'er body to eny well-appointed man who warnts to 'ave a look at it.

DREAMER. These quiet, Christian maenads bind the hands to blast the minds with yearning.

BISHOP'S SISTER'S VOICE (*calling shrilly and imperatively to the water-fowl*). Chuck chuck, chuck chuck chuck chuck!

ATHEIST (*indicating a bench with a gesture*). Sit dahn 'ere a second?

DREAMER. Righto.

(*They sit down.*)

ATHEIST. Then, when the kid was six or seven, crowned with paper orange blossoms over a white veil, the mother marries a heavy dragoon home from the front on leave; 'as a star-lit time with the warrior for a week; 'ad an allowance flung at 'er from the Government, which grew into a pension when 'er dragoon disappeared in one of those hail en' farewell advances from the front line.

DREAMER. Home they brought her warrior dead—hard lines on the bride.

ATHEIST. She soon wandered aht of the shadows. It was only when 'er 'air grew grey, en' the wrinkles budded on 'er fice; en' she 'ad 'ad enough of me, en' I 'ad 'ad enough of 'er, that she began to sing the prises en' mourn the loss of 'er dead dragoon.

DREAMER. How did she fasten on to you?

ATHEIST. To give 'er 'er doo, it was me fastened on to 'er first. When I met 'er, she was the kind of woman'd mike a man stand up en' long for something to 'appen—you know, Dreamer?

DREAMER. Know? Oh, indeed I do—too damn well!

ATHEIST. When I fahnd aut abaht the kid, en' where she was, I tripped off to the nuns; said I was the father, en' after a five weeks' fight, brought the kid 'ome agine. Then I 'ad a job with 'er. They must 'ave 'ad 'er pickled in 'oly water. I did my best to show 'er rahnd a bit; took awye 'eaven from over 'er' ead, en' 'ell awye from under 'er feet; but the nuns 'ad got their claws in 'er deep, for 'er little mind was rotten with the fear of 'ell!

DREAMER (*bitterly*). I know! They cancel life with their livid love of God!

ATHEIST. Everything went well for a long time. Missus's pension en' my wyges as a carpenter kept things going hale en' hearty. We gyve the kid a good educytion, en' I taught 'er a lot of things myself. But when the kid was stretching towards womanhood, the old woman began to 'ite the girl, en' tike to drink, coming dahn to wherever I was a working en' chising me in a drunken fury aht of the job.

DREAMER. A golden hour of life for the young lady! Go on.

ATHEIST. She's often come into the shop where I was working, asked for money, en' when she didn't get it, grabbed up a sawr or en 'ammer, en' chised me rahnd the benches! Chised me rahnd en' rahnd, shouting aht that I forced 'er to tike to drink, en' that I mide 'er continually go abaht in fear of 'er life!

DREAMER. Why didn't you knock her down?

ATHEIST. Oh, I couldn't rise my 'and to a woman, Dreamer.

DREAMER. Not even when she had a hammer in her hand?

ATHEIST. Specially 'er when she 'ad a 'ammer

in 'er 'and. Worse cime after: she began to mourn the memory of 'er 'usband. She began to manufacture wreaths of laurel leaves en' scarlet poppies, completing a new one weekly, en' dumping each on a different memorial, en' choosing a different dye in the week for her visit to one. After a long time of patient endoorance, one dye the girl suddenly ups en', withaht a word, goes. A few months lyter, I goes, too, so 'ere she is, a fire novitiate in the practice of profyne love, en' 'ere I am, a speaker in the Pawk against Gord, 'ell, 'eaven, en' kindred superstitions.

(*They sit silent and thoughtful. The two* CHAIR ATTENDANTS *enter, one from the left and the other from the right, crossing each other as before. They snort with anger when they see the chairs lying flat on the ground. They lift them up and replace them in correct positions on the sward.*)

OLDER ONE (*angrily*). Demned kids agine! If I only 'ad one of 'em across my knee, I'd knock the abundant 'ilarity aht of 'im.

(*A heavily built and plain-looking* POLICEWOMAN *saunters in, glances at the two men on the bench, then stops to say a word to the* OLDER CHAIR ATTENDANT.)

POLICEWOMAN (*to* OLDER ATTENDANT). 'Ow's the poor old leg, to-day, Basil?

OLDER ONE (*dolefully*). Creaking a little for the last few dyes, constable, creaking a bit.

(*The* BISHOP *comes up from the lakeside, followed stiffly, at a distance, by his* SISTER, *who stands watching her* BROTHER *with a stiff and troubled look on her face, as he talks to the others.*)

BISHOP (*breezily to all*). Hello, boys! Good-morning, constable.

ATTENDANTS (*responding breezily together*). 'ello, sir!

POLICEWOMAN (*with a dignified salute*). 'Morning, sir.

BISHOP (*buoyantly*). Glorious nip of crispness in the air of a Spring morning, isn't there?

POLICEWOMAN. Exhilaryting, I'd sy, sir.

OLDER ONE (*gaily*). Gets you going, ri' enough.

YOUNGER ONE (*affecting gaiety*). Dideray, dideree, diderum.

BISHOP. Makes life feel less, er, cock-eyed. The flowers appear on the earth; the time of the singing of birds is come, and the voice of the turtle is heard in the land—God speaking of Spring, friends.

POLICEWOMAN. Quate, sir.

YOUNGER ONE. 'Its it off nacely, sir.

DREAMER (*to the* BISHOP). Not God, but a poet speaking of Spring, sir. Render to God the things that are God's and to the poet the things that are his.

BISHOP (*to the* DREAMER—*smilingly*). God is in all, and God is all things, sir.

ATHEIST (*combatively*). Would the reverend en' learned gentleman tell us poor people 'oo is Gord, wot 'e is, en' where 'e is locyted?

POLICEWOMAN (*to the* ATHEIST, *stiffly*). You keep your almighty arguments for your meetings.

OLDER ONE (*viciously*). 'Ear, 'ear!

BISHOP (*to* POLICEWOMAN—*graciously*). Never mind, constable; there are always those who never will give thanks to God for life.

DREAMER. Always, when there are those who have no life for which to thank Him.

YOUNGER ONE (*encouragingly to the* BISHOP). Never mind 'im, sir—go on torking abaht the Spring;—Dideree, dideray, diderum;—and the birds!

(*The birds begin to sing more merrily.*)

BISHOP (*joyously*). Listen! The busy birds warbling a sylvan sonata. Facing out life with a song! No shaking of the head here, in denial of God's goodness and glory. Sursum corda! Lift up your hearts.

DREAMER. We lift them up unto the birds.

OLDER ONE (*gushingly*). The birds bring a man 'ope. Even with the doo 'eavy on the grass, a feller begins to feel spry en' elevyted when they stert their chirruping.

POLICEWOMAN. Not a daht abaht it.

BISHOP'S SISTER. Gilbert, come and look at the swans.

BISHOP (*with conviction—to the* POLICEWOMAN). Do you know, constable, that, to an observing mind, it seems to be conclusive that the most beautiful part of God's creation—apart from man, of course——

POLICEWOMAN. Quate — setting man en' woman aside for a moment.

BISHOP. Quite. The most beautiful part of God's manifold creation is, undoubtedly, the birds!

(*The* BISHOP *lifts his head and looks up at the sky; then the* POLICEWOMAN *does the same, and, lastly, the two* CHAIR ATTENDANTS *lift their heads and crane their necks in an upward look.*)

BISHOP. Brave little birds.

POLICEWOMAN. Beautiful little birds.

THE TWO CHAIR ATTENDANTS (*together*). Beautiful, innocent, little birds.

(*They all lower their heads again—first the*

BISHOP, *then the* POLICEWOMAN, *and, lastly, the* CHAIR ATTENDANTS.)

YOUNGER ONE (*enthusiastically*). Reminds a man that Gord watches even over the fall of the sparrer! Dideray, dideree, diderum.

ATHEIST (*jeeringly*). Ay, en' the fall of the 'awk on the sparrer to tear it to pieces.

(*The* OLDER ATTENDANT *limps over to the* ATHEIST *till he is facing him, glowering at him for a moment before he speaks.*)

OLDER ONE (*hotly*). You shut your rotten mouth, will you? Warnt to 'ear yourself torkin', torkin', do you? Try to look at things in perspective, carn't you? Wot's you or me in the general scheme of things, eh? Speck of dust, blide of grass, a nought, a nothing. Wish Jimmie Douglas of the *Sundye Express* was 'ere en' 'eard you. 'E's the man would stun the pire of you into a stiff jest. (*To* YOUNGER ATTENDANT) Wot d'you sye, Godfrey?

YOUNGER ONE. 'E's a man as knows 'oo's 'oo en' wot's wot.

OLDER ONE. You bet 'e does. 'Ow, on a 'olidye, sitting by the sea, under the stars, wot 'e sawr, en' wot 'e 'eard? 'Ow 'e marvelled at the star dust 'e could see, en' the star dust 'e couldn't see; en' 'ow 'e was filled with terror en' fear as 'e 'eard the clock of eternity ticking!

BISHOP'S SISTER (*testily*). Come, come along, dear, and let us look at the swans.

DREAMER (*to* OLDER ATTENDANT). It won't be long, old man, till you hear the clock of eternity ticking.

OLDER ONE (*stormily*). Well, wot if it won't? It ain't the end, is it?

DREAMER (*fervently*). Kill off the old and stupid, O God, who, having nothing to give, have nothing to get!

OLDER ONE (*violently*). Thinking that life doesn't keep agoing on when it ends! I yells it aht, I yells it aht with Jimmie Douglas—death's only the gitewye to a fuller en' a nobler life!

(*A* YOUNG MAN IN PLUS-FOURS *enters, right, looking behind him as he comes in. He glances at all who are present, then goes up path in centre, and appears on the slope above, looking to the right, then to the left, and then to the right again.*)

BISHOP (*up to the* YOUNG MAN IN PLUS-FOURS —*genially*). Lovely view out over the lake and all, from where you're standing, friend.

(*The* YOUNG MAN IN PLUS-FOURS *takes no notice of the* BISHOP'S *remark.*)

BISHOP (*again*). Lovely view out over the

lake and all, from where you're standing, friend.

(*The* YOUNG MAN IN PLUS-FOURS *takes no notice.*

The SCARLET WOMAN *enters from below, passes by the group on the sward, and goes up centre path, leading to the slope. She is dressed in red, with a crescent in black on her right hip. She wears a black hat, having on one side of it a little crescent in red. Her face is stiffened with a stylised smile.*

A silence falls on the group as they realise what she is, and the POLICEWOMAN *eyes her keenly as she goes by.*

The SCARLET WOMAN *goes past the* YOUNG MAN IN PLUS-FOURS, *swinging her hips and sticking out her bottom as she goes out.*

After a moment or two, the YOUNG MAN IN PLUS-FOURS *follows her out.*

The POLICEWOMAN *strolls up the centre path, and follows the* YOUNG MAN IN PLUS-FOURS.

The BISHOP *looks stupid and the* ATHEIST *laughs ironically.*

The Birds give a special burst of song.)

ATHEIST (*to the* DREAMER). Thinks 'e was admiring the view. (*To the* BISHOP) Couldn't you see 'e was 'unting for a fawncy frill? Sweet supplement to the dyely service!

BISHOP'S SISTER (*impatiently pulling the* BISHOP *by the arm towards the path by the lake*). For goodness' sake, Gilbert, come along and look at the swans.

ATHEIST (*getting up from the bench*). 'E's a better charnce with the swans than 'e 'as with us. Getting cold sitting 'ere, en' I've gotta go to the Library to look over agine *The Origin of the Idea of a God*. (*To the* DREAMER). Coming a bit of the wye?

DREAMER. No; gotta song shaping in my head—Song of the Down-and-Outs—and I must try to think it out. Had a good collection at last night's meeting;—see you at one in the old place, and we'll have some ham and a cup of what's called coffee.

ATHEIST (*cheerfully*). I'll be there before the second pip sahnds. (*To the* CHAIR ATTENDANTS) Cheerio, Samson en' Delilah.

(*He bows mockingly to the* CHAIR ATTENDANTS, *who sniff with indignation, and, crossing by each other, go out, one to the right, and the other to the left.*

The ATHEIST *goes up centre path, crosses slope, and goes out as—*

Two good-looking NURSEMAIDS, *wheeling*

prams, enter, and cross over. One of them stops to arrange the clothes over the baby in the pram she is wheeling.

The DREAMER *takes a note-book from his pocket and is about to write in it, when his attention is attracted to the* NURSEMAIDS.

A YOUNG GUARDSMAN *appears on the slope at the left corner, and the* GARDENER, *with a pair of shears in his hand, at the right corner of the slope, both looking down at the maids.*

The GUARDSMAN *chirrups down to the* NURSEMAIDS, *who hear, but ostentatiously take no notice.*)

1ST NURSEMAID. I think she's awfully stuck up, since she sterted to tike rahnd a countess's byby.

2ND NURSEMAID. I must sye I didn't find 'er so. One dye she let me wheel the pram from one end of the pawk to the other.

1ST NURSEMAID (*with surprise*). En' the countess's kid in the cer?

2ND NURSEMAID. Of course.

1ST NURSEMAID. Well, that was kind of 'er, I must admit.

(*The* DREAMER *chirrups shyly and faintly to the* MAIDS.)

2ND NURSEMAID (*with a scornful glance at the* DREAMER). Tike no notice. En' she showed me every stitch 'er little lydyship 'ad on 'er, so that mistress could get en exact copy of everything.

1ST NURSEMAID (*in astonishment*). G'wye?

2ND NURSEMAID. Yep.

1ST NURSEMAID (*emphatically*). Well, that was kind of 'er, I must admit.

(*The* GARDENER *chirrups to the two* NURSEMAIDS.)

1ST NURSEMAID (*with an indignant toss of her head*). Tike no notice of 'im.

2ND NURSEMAID (*arranging the clothes in the pram*). People my sye wot they like, but it is a countess's byby en' that is a considerytion.

(*The* THREE MEN *chirrup together down to the* MAIDS, *who, with an indignant look at the men, go off swiftly.*

The DREAMER *looks after them, then begins to write in a note-book.*

The GUARDSMAN *comes down slowly, and follows the* MAIDS; *the* GARDENER *disappears behind some bushes, but the sound of the shears clipping the bushes can be heard, and, occasionally, his head can be seen above them.*

The BOY *runs in again and knocks down*

the chairs that the ATTENDANTS *have arranged. He is running out left, when he meets the* OLDER ATTENDANT; *he turns and runs to the right, to meet the* YOUNGER ATTENDANT. *They make for the* BOY, *but their lameness prevent them from success. He dodges them and escapes along the slope.*

The DREAMER *enjoys the sport.*

The TWO ATTENDANTS *lift up the chairs and replace them in position again.*

The DREAMER *watches them dreamily.*)

OLDER ONE (*savagely*). Kids in this Pawk mike a man feel dinegerous; curse of 'ell on the whole of 'em!

YOUNGER ONE. All kids 'as a 'abit of knocking things abaht.

OLDER ONE (*furiously*). 'Abit! It's a maniar, man, a maniar. See the slightest rip in a thing —tear it in two, tear it in two! See the merest crack in a thing—smash it up, en' smash it to pieces—curse of 'ell on the whole of 'em!

(*The* DREAMER *goes up to the slope and watches the* GARDENER *working.*)

YOUNGER ONE (*after a pause*). Sawr the boss torking to you—complyning?

OLDER ONE. Ever eny other wye? Sawr 'im torking to you—complyning?

YOUNGER ONE (*gloomily*). Sime old yarn—not quick enough on the pins.

OLDER ONE (*irritably*). Let's forgit it.

(*A short pause.*)

YOUNGER ONE (*with an attempt at brightness*). Listened to the wireless las' night.

OLDER ONE. 'Eard enything worth while?

YOUNGER ONE. Pageant of England—wunnerful, wunnerful.

OLDER ONE. Wot was it abaht?

YOUNGER ONE. Orl abaht the old guys as used to be kings—you know—en' stitesmen 'oo mide the Empire wot it is.

OLDER ONE (*scornfully*). Don't 'old with them things; let bygones be bygones, I says. 'Ot jazz's wot I likes—something to keep the mind from gitting aht of dite.

YOUNGER ONE (*proudly*). We carn't afford to forgit the things wot mide us wot we are. Mide me thrill to 'ear the sahnd of Drike's drum, it did!

OLDER ONE. 'Oo's drum?

YOUNGER ONE. Drike's drum; the bloke 'oo left 'is gime of bowls, en' 'opped aht in 'is galloon to smash the Armyda: the sahnd of it mide a man feel prahde to be en Englishman!

(*The* ATTENDANTS *suddenly stiffen their bodies and listen intently, their faces paling as they stare in front of them.*

The DREAMER *rises and moves back almost out of view.*

In the distance are heard faint sounds of sombre music, saddened with the intermingled beats of a muffled drum.)

TWO ATTENDANTS (*together*). The drum beat en' chant of the Down-en'-Outs!

1ST ATTENDANT (*tensely, to his companion*). Wot'r you stiffening for?

2ND ATTENDANT (*as tensely*). Wot'r you styring at?

1ST ATTENDANT / 2ND ATTENDANT (*together*). I wasn't styring. / I wasn't stiffening.

1ST ATTENDANT. Didja 'ear enything?

2ND ATTENDANT. No, nothing, did you?

1ST ATTENDANT. Nothing.

(*They go by each other, one to the left, the other to the right, and go slowly out, a deeper limp coming into each man's lame leg, keeping time to the distant chant and drum beat.*

The DREAMER *is watching the* GARDENER *arranging the daffodils. The* BISHOP *and his* SISTER *appear round the path leading from the lake, followed by a loud quacking from the waterfowl.*)

DREAMER (*to the* GARDENER). Happy man to

be handling the scented purple, blue, and yellow of the blossoms.

GARDENER (*indifferently*). Let them live and let them die, for I'm not thinking of blossoms now.

DREAMER. What are you thinking of, then?

GARDENER. Of a dance I take a sweet heifer to when the sun goes in and the stars come out.

DREAMER. I envy you the fondling of a flower by day, and of a girl by night.

GARDENER (*gleefully*). After the dance, we go to her flat to spend the night in a foam and sweat of joy.

DREAMER (*musingly*). He brought me home to his house of wine, and his banner over me was love.

(*The* BISHOP *and his* SISTER *have come from the lakeside path, and stop beside the* GARDENER *on their way out.*)

BISHOP (*breezily—to the* GARDENER). Beautiful flowers, Tom, beautiful flowers.

BISHOP'S SISTER. Their gold would do to gild the robes of Gabriel.

BISHOP (*softly and reverently*). They bring one nearer to the great Creator, Tom.

GARDENER. Ned, sir, Ned.

BISHOP. Yes, of course: Ned. They bring us near to heaven, Tom,—eh, Ned.

GARDENER. Yessir, quite.

DREAMER (*to the* BISHOP). I'm afraid Ned is thinking only of spending to-night abed in the arms of a pretty heifer.

BISHOP'S SISTER (*coldly indignant*). Come along, Gilbert; come away, please.

BISHOP (*in confusion as he is led away by his* SISTER). Quite—no, no. Yes—Oh no! Good-night, Tom, eh, Ned—no, Bill.

(*The* BISHOP *and his* SISTER *pass over slope and go off*.)

GARDENER. That made them fade out. Wish the night was here. The sun seems to halt in the heavens. She thinks I'll marry her when I'm fixed on the staff, but I don't fancy marriage. Mad to have a kid—matrimony's signature song. Not for me, though.

DREAMER (*musingly*). I hear a song in what we've said.

GARDENER (*surprised*). A song in what?

DREAMER. Heaven, the flowers, and a girl.

GARDENER (*looking at him in wonder*). Oh, do you?

(*The* DREAMER *takes a note-book from his pocket, reclines down on the grass near the daffodils in such a way that he is almost hidden. He thinks for a moment then he begins to write.*

The GARDENER *arranges the daffodils so that the* DREAMER *is hidden.*

A pause, then the GARDENER *begins to sing.*)

GARDENER (*singing*):

I'm not thinking of blossoms at all, but only of the slow ending of day;
Then I'll dance with a girl in a hall, when the sinking sun says it's the end of the day.
All sweet-scented blossoms long thoughts can recall,
Fair in their bloom, and sweet still in their fall,
Bloom afresh and with pride hidden under a shawl.
I'm not thinking of blossoms at all—
Let them flourish and die in their old-fashion'd way;
For I'll dance with a girl in a hall,
At the end, at the end, at the ending of day!

I'm not thinking of heaven at all, but only of the slow ending of day;
Then I'll dance with a girl in a hall, when the sinking sun says it's the end of the day.
Words of the gospel on deafen'd ears fall,
And the joy of the saints is a joy that is small
To the joy and the joys nestling under a shawl.
I'm not thinking of heaven at all—it's a dying out star a long distance away;—

For I'll dance with a girl in a hall,
At the end, at the end, at the ending of day?

(*At the start of the second verse of the song,* COUPLES, *linking arms, enter from different points and mix, cross by each other, parading about, and keeping time to the lilt of the tune. As the second verse of the song ends, the* GARDENER *moves back among the crowd and goes off, leaving the last verse of the song to be sung by the* COUPLES *parading about the scene.*

Before the last verse has been begun, the two placarded EVANGELISTS *enter, one from the right, the other from the left, and dolefully walk about with bent heads among the crowd. Each man has a placard on back and breast. Each placard has a text printed on it in black and red lettering. On the placards borne by the* 1ST EVANGELIST *are the texts, "The Wicked shall be turned into Hell", on the front placard; and on the back, "Repent Ye". On the placards carried by the* 2ND EVANGELIST *are the texts: "Man is Appointed to Die", and "After Death, the Judgment".*

The 1ST EVANGELIST *has a lemon-shaped head, staring, stupid-looking eyes, shrunken cheeks, scowling lines round a wide mouth, and ears that stick out from the side of his head.*

The 2ND EVANGELIST *has a big head, coarse face, heavy hanging lips, and a snubby nose. He has a habit of frequently blinking his eyes, and he turns his feet out. Both are shabbily dressed. They amble about among the crowd, but no notice is taken of them.*

The parading COUPLES *singing*:)

Since poor Adam first ventur'd to fall,
And Eve took a hand in the venturesome game,
Life's banner's turn'd into a shawl,
Deep fring'd in desire and spear-pointed with flame.
Let the pray'r-busy Bishop akneel in his stall,
Drone deep in a measur'd, liturgical drawl,
That the pleasures of love are all sweeten'd with gall:—
I and the crowd don't believe it at all,—
Desire for a woman's both worship and play;
And so I'll dance with a girl in a hall,
At the end, at the end, at the ending of day!

(*While this verse is being sung, the* YOUNG

WHORE *enters hurriedly, but without spoiling the ordered movements of the singers, and mixes with the crowd, passing in and out between several couples. She has a preoccupied and rather anxious look on her face, and appears to be searching for someone.*

She is very pretty, and her figure would make most young men immediately forget the seventh commandment. Her face is a little pale, but this paleness is hidden by a cautious and clever make-up. She has an intelligent look, which is becoming a little worn by contact with the selfishness and meanness of the few clients that have patronised her; for these, though unable to resist the desire to have her, hate her subconsciously before they go with her, and consciously detest her when their desires have been satisfied. She has read a little, but not enough; she has thought a little, but not enough; she is deficient in self-assurance, and is too generous and sensitive to be a clever whore, and her heart is not in the business.

Convent tales of punishments reserved for the particular sins tangled round sex expression have left in her mind lusty images of hell fire. She is dressed in black with a scarlet hat. On the hat is an ornament in black, of a crescent; and the hip of the black skirt is decorated with a scarlet crescent. When she has moved about for a few moments, she hurries up the centre, crosses the slope almost at a run, and goes out in the middle of the singing, following the direction taken by the ATHEIST.

After the singing of the last verse, all go off, with the exception of a GUARDSMAN, *the* 1ST NURSEMAID, *and the* TWO EVANGELISTS. *The* GUARDSMAN *and the* 1ST NURSEMAID *settle down on the bench for a sweet time.*

During the singing of the CROWD, *the mouths of the* EVANGELISTS *have been moving, but the hearty singing of the* COUPLES *prevented the words of what they sang from being heard. After a glance around, they amble over to the* COUPLE *sitting on the bench, and, almost leaning over them, continue their song in weak, piping voices, plainly directing its meaning to the* GUARDSMAN *and the* NURSEMAID.)

1ST EVANGELIST (*bawling the words to any kind of tune*):
Hear the warning without; heed the warning within;
That soul shall be lost that dies lost in its sin!

2ND EVANGELIST (*singing*):
Is it well with thy soul?

1ST EVANGELIST (*singing*):
Yes, it's well with my soul.

BOTH TOGETHER:
Is it well,—yes it's well with my soul!

(*The* GUARDSMAN *and the* 1ST NURSEMAID *have listened to this admonitory hymn in dismay, and now, hastily, get up from the bench, and hurry off, followed by the* EVANGELISTS *droning their doggerel, as the* ATHEIST *enters, with the* YOUNG WHORE, *pale, frightened-looking, and panting sharply, leaning heavily on his arm.*)

YOUNG WHORE (*anxiously*). I'll sit down on a seat, dad, for a minute. My legs are giving under me; let me sit down a second.

ATHEIST (*irritably, as he leads her to a seat*). You'll be all right in a second. Shouldn't 'ave rushed en' rushed the wye you did. En' 'urry up. I've gotta go to the library en' read *The Origin of the Idea of a God.*

YOUNG WHORE (*between breaths*). I was afraid, if I didn't run, I'd lose sight of you, and I wanted to see you.

ATHEIST (*as he helps the* YOUNG WHORE *to sit down*). Damn stupid to rush yourself into a heart attack.

YOUNG WHORE (*frightened*). There's a shadow passing over my eyes again! (*Grasping the* ATHEIST's *arm*) Dad, I'm afraid I'm far from well.

ATHEIST (*soothingly*). Just a little flutter from over exertion, that's all. All our hearts jump at times.

YOUNG WHORE (*vehemently*). I tell you it's deeper than that, an' I'll croak suddenly, sooner or later. The other night I had a man with me, an' when I was half stripped it came on me as he was coming over to paw me. In a mist I saw the fright in his eyes, saw him huddling his clothes on an' hurrying away. Then I fell down. In a faint I fell down, till the morning came an' brought up the woman below to find me still in a faint where I fell down.

ATHEIST. Excitement, over-excitement. Did the boyo leave his fee behind him?

YOUNG WHORE (*hysterically*). If I have to die, I'll die game; I'll die dancing!

ATHEIST (*reprovingly*). Shush, not so loud; we're in a park.

YOUNG WHORE (*persuasively catching hold of the* ATHEIST'S *arm*). I want you to help me, dad; I'll go mad if I have to live alone any longer.

ATHEIST (*firmly*). No, no; no more of that. Live your own life. I'm not your father, so cut out the daddy business.

YOUNG WHORE (*moving closer to him*). You crept into a father's place when you took me away from the nuns who were moulding my life round the sin of my mother. You made me call you dad when you took me away from their crosses, their crowns, and their canes, and lifted my hands up in salute to the sun and the moon and the stars. (*Putting an arm round him*) You'll give me one more chance, won't you? You will, you will.

ATHEIST (*restlessly*). I did that twice before, and as soon as you felt well, you hurried off, leaving me with rooms I didn't want, and furniture I couldn't sell.

YOUNG WHORE (*leaning wearily against his shoulder*). I can't live alone any longer, dad. When I lie down in bed and stretch out in search of sleep, the darkness reddens into a glow from the fire that can never be quenched.

Green-eyed, barrel-bellied men glare and grin at me; huge-headed, yellow-eyed women beckon to me out of the glow from the fire that can never be quenched. Black-feathered owls, with eyes like great white moons, peck at me as they fly through the glow from the fire that can never be quenched. Save me, dad, oh save me!

ATHEIST (*with a scornful sigh of resignation*). The hell en' red-fire-forever talk of the nuns! Framing the world 'en filling life with it till we eat, sleep, work, play en' go awhoring in the smoke of hell!

YOUNG WHORE (*humbly*). It will only be for a little while, dad, for I'm going to marry the Gardener.

ATHEIST (*with a movement of impatience*). Oh, for Gord's sike, put 'im aht of your 'ead, girl. He 'as as much intention of marrying you as I 'ave.

YOUNG WHORE. We're going to a dance together to-night, when we'll settle everything. You'll see.

ATHEIST (*convincingly*). I know 'im—a boyo that'll never keep a cow while 'e can get a penn'orth of milk.

(*A handsome young* SALVATION ARMY OFFICER *enters from the right above, crosses slope, and comes down towards a seat some distance away from the* YOUNG WHORE *and the* ATHEIST. *He is trying to read a book as he walks along. He is wearing a yellow mackintosh, which is open, showing the blue jersey of a Staff Officer. The* OFFICER *glances at the* YOUNG WHORE *as he passes, and she returns the look. He sits down on a seat and steals a furtive look at the* YOUNG WHORE. *He meets her eyes and lowers his glance to the ground. He again glances at her, at her face, and then at her legs.)*

YOUNG WHORE (*turning her thoughts away from the* OFFICER, *and pressing close to the* ATHEIST, *as she puts an arm coaxingly round his neck*). You'll do what I ask you, this once, dad, only this once, won't you?

ATHEIST (*firmly removing her arm from around his neck*). No, never again. Swing along on your own sweet way, and leave your dad out of it.

YOUNG WHORE (*tensely*). You won't? You won't, dad?

ATHEIST (*in a tone of finality*). No, I won't!

(*There is a pause, during which the* YOUNG WHORE, *with tightened lips and a sullen look in her eyes, looks in front of her.*)

YOUNG WHORE (*thrusting her face close to that of the* ATHEIST). I believe in God, see? An' in the beginning He created the heaven an' the earth.

ATHEIST (*moving his face away from the* YOUNG WHORE'S). I see, I see.

(*The* SALVATION ARMY OFFICER *is listening intently to what is being said.*)

YOUNG WHORE (*following the face of the* ATHEIST *with her own—vehemently*). An' in the resurrection of the dead, when they that have done good shall go into life everlasting, and they that have done evil into everlasting fire!

(*The* ATHEIST *rises from his seat without a word, and turning up the centre path, crosses the slope and passes out.*)

YOUNG WHORE (*rising and speaking loudly after the* ATHEIST). An' I believe that God's near them who need His help, an' helps them who ask His help—see?

(*She sinks down on the seat again, and begins to cry softly and resentfully.*

The SALVATION ARMY OFFICER, *after a moment's hesitation, comes over, looks with a shy interest at the pretty legs displayed by a disarranged skirt, then sits down beside her.*)

S.A. OFFICER (*earnestly*). No need to cry, sister, for no one trusts to God in vain.

YOUNG WHORE (*resentfully*). Oh, go away; I'm miserable, for he that's gone is the only real friend I have in the world.

S.A. OFFICER. God is your only friend.

YOUNG WHORE. I've not called upon Him for years, and He will not hasten to hear me now.

S.A. OFFICER (*putting his hand gently on her knee*). God would empty heaven of His angels rather than let the humblest penitent perish.

YOUNG WHORE (*in low tones*). If I ask for help, will He hear?

S.A. OFFICER. He will hear.

YOUNG WHORE. And hearing, will He listen?

S.A. OFFICER. Hearing, He will listen.

YOUNG WHORE (*grasping his arm appealingly*). And listening, will He grant what the sinner asks, to save the sinner from a life of sin?

S.A. OFFICER (*fervently, as he caresses her knee*). God is able to save to the uttermost all them that come to Him.

YOUNG WHORE (*earnestly, after a few moments' thought*). I'll pray and pray and pray till all that's done's annulled, and all that is to do is blessed by God's agreement.

S.A. OFFICER (*softly*). Praise the Lord!

YOUNG WHORE (*becoming conscious that he is caressing her knee*). Oh God, don't do that, please! You'll make a ladder, and silk stockings aren't easy to get.

(*She pushes his hand away, pulls down her skirt, and looks at him questioningly. He stands up, embarrassed, and fidgets with his cap.*)

S.A. OFFICER (*a little nervously*). I must go on to our meeting. Will you come? (*She shakes her head.*) No? Some other time. I should like to keep in touch with you. Very much indeed. (*He half extends his hand to her, then draws it back.*) Good-bye.

YOUNG WHORE (*in a formal voice*). Good-bye.

(*He turns up the centre path, looks back for a moment at the* YOUNG WHORE, *then crosses the slope and goes out.*

The YOUNG WHORE *remains sitting thoughtfully on the seat.*

The GARDENER *comes in, carrying a slender, black-painted maypole which he fixes in the ground near the centre. On the top of the pole is a hoop from which hang long green and dark yellow ribbons. The* YOUNG WHORE *raises her head and sees the* GARDENER. *She runs to him and flings her arms around his neck.*)

GARDENER (*astonished*). What has you here? Aren't you working?

YOUNG WHORE. No, I've given it up.

GARDENER. Why?

YOUNG WHORE. You know well enough, you know well enough. How often have I told you that the swine of a manager brings good-looking girls, one at a time, to a silent store-room to sort chemises, and then sends his slimy paw flickering around under their skirts. When he made a clutch at me, I came away.

GARDENER (*peevishly*). Oh, you should have fenced him off as every girl does with a man like that. What are you going to do if you can't get another job?

YOUNG WHORE (*coaxingly*). That's why I wanted to speak to you. You'll have to live with me; I'm frightened, I'm frightened to live alone any longer.

GARDENER (*suspiciously*). Live with you—how live with you?

YOUNG WHORE (*with calm confidence*). Marry me, Ned. You want me, or you do not want me. I'm not going to be just a dance number for you any longer. Do you want me or do you not?

GARDENER (*nervously*). Look here, Jannice, the foreman's knocking around, an' if he catches me idle I'll be in want of a job too.

YOUNG WHORE (*insisting*). Do you want me or do you not want me?

GARDENER (*evasively*). 'Course I want you; but we can talk about this to-night, darling.

YOUNG WHORE (*firmly*). No, now; what we say now will last our lives out. There will only be our two selves—we needn't have a kid till we can afford one. (*Suddenly putting her arms round him*) You will, you will, Ned; this means everything to me, everything, everything!

(*The* FOREMAN *appears above, and stands watching them with a leer on his face. He is a short, wizened-faced man of fifty. He is wearing an apron-trousered suit of dungarees, which is here and there splashed with mud. Round his neck is a fresh, white, stiff collar and gaudy coloured tie; and on his head he wears a high-crowned, new-looking bowler hat.*)

GARDENER (*frightened—trying to remove her arms*). Oh, be sensible for God's sake; we can't talk of these things here.

YOUNG WHORE (*vehemently*). Oh, be a man, Ned, be a man, and if you want a thing, take a little risk to get it! Answer me—is it yes or no?

FOREMAN (*speaking down to them*). 'Ere, you do your courtin' ahtside of werkin' hours, see? You're not pide for agitytin' the lydies. (*Loudly*) 'Ear me torkin' to you?

GARDENER (*up to the* FOREMAN). Yes, sir.

YOUNG WHORE (*a little hysterically*). Oh, tell the old, wizened last-look-at-life to go to hell, Ned!

FOREMAN (*speaking angrily down to them*). Tell 'er to skip, will you? No 'eifers, time or wild, allowed in this 'ere camp. You're only 'angin' on to your job as it is, so tell 'er to skip, quick!

GARDENER (*roughly trying to release himself from the* YOUNG WHORE'S *hold*). Buzz off, will you? I'll see you to-night, I tell you.

YOUNG WHORE (*violently*). Answer the question I put to you—yes or no, yes or no, yes or no!

GARDENER (*with a shout*). No!

(*The* YOUNG WHORE *looks silently at him for a moment, then turns away, and sits down on a seat at the back. She has a tense look on her face, though her lips are quivering.*

The MAN IN PLUS-FOURS *enters, gives her a meaning look as he passes, and going up the path, crosses slope, gives her another look, and goes out.*

After a moment's pause, she rises, and, without looking at the GARDENER, *follows the* MAN IN PLUS-FOURS.

The FOREMAN *comes toward the* GARDENER *in a slow and grim manner.*)

FOREMAN (*as he comes down to the* GARDENER). All this 'oney-suckle en' the bee business is to be forgotten till after knockin'-off time, see? You know we 'as to be ready in en hour for them blarsted fools en' their folk darnces. So get a move on, see? In your own time you can charnce your awm as much as you like with dandy women, randy women, candy women, ready women, heady women, steady women, beddy women, weddy women, splendid women, mended women, ended women, boyish women, toyish women, coyish women (*he has started to go away, and keeps talking as he goes*), fancy women, dancy women, chancy women, or eny other clarss of women you warnt to 'andle or leggle. (*Shouting at him*) Oh, lettin' it in through one ear en' aht through the other—are you?

GARDENER (*humbly*). No, sir, oh no, sir.

FOREMAN (*roughly—as he goes out*). No, sir, oh no, sir—get a move on then.

(*The* GARDENER *looks sullenly after the*

FOREMAN, *then stands with bent head, thinking despondently, thoughtlessly pulling ribbons through his hand.*

On the slope appears the YOUNG WHORE, *crying softly, closely followed by the* POLICEWOMAN.)

POLICEWOMAN (*complacently*). I caught you in the act that time, me lyedy.

YOUNG WHORE (*sobbing softly*). It was he spoke to me, miss; on my word of honour, it was he spoke to me first.

POLICEWOMAN (*sarcastically*). On your word of honour! Tell the magistrite that when you're in front of 'im. If I'm eny kind of a guesser, you'll not solicit eny more young en' innocent men for a month to come. Go on.

(*They pass out.*)

The GARDENER *has looked up and comprehends all that has happened.*

He turns his face away and timidly and nervously continues to pull the ribbon through his hand, as

THE GATES CLOSE

SCENE II

Summer Noon.

The same as the preceding scene on a noonday in Summer. The green is a richer and darker colour and the sky is a glittering blue. The steel-helmeted soldier, in the sparkle of the sun, looks like a figure of gleaming steel. At the end of the path leading round the lake, occasional glimpses of the red, black, or yellow sails of one-man-managed yachts can be caught as the vessels pass by. The cries of the waterfowl and the gulls are now softer, for food is plentiful. Instead of the daffodils, the slope is ornamented now with a clump of hollyhocks, yellow, white, red; and with these colours are mingled the lovely blue of a clump of cornflowers. People are moving about.

The DREAMER *enters as the gates are opening and passes through them into the Park. He is gazing at a piece of white paper, held in his left hand, with an intense look on his face.*

His right hand beats time gently, as he murmurs the tune of the opening chorus. People are moving about as he crosses over and goes out. They are all gay, and move with a sensuous enjoyment of the loveliness of the day. A few in bathing costumes stroll about among the others. As the DREAMER *goes out, portion of the crowd begin to sing, and are joined by the rest when the chorus of the song comes.*

SOME OF THE CROWD:

Ye who are haggard and giddy with care, busy counting your profit and losses,
Showing the might of your name unto God in the gay-coloured page of a cheque book;
Storing the best of your life in a drawer of your desk at the office:

ALL TOGETHER:

Bellow good-bye to the buggerin' lot 'n come out
To bow down the head 'n bend down the knee to the bee, the bird, 'n the blossom,
Bann'ring the breast of the earth with a wonderful beauty!

SOME OF THE CROWD:

Ye who are twisting a prayer from your thoughts in the dimness 'n gloom of the churches,

Lighting your candle-petitions away to chalk-
 coloured virgins and martyrs,
Racking your life for a hope of a cosy corner in
 heaven:

ALL THE CROWD TOGETHER:

Bellow, etc.

SOME OF THE CROWD:

Ye who in senates, 'n Parliaments talk, talk on
 through the day 'n the night-time,
Talk, 'n still talk, 'n still talk, 'n talk on through
 the hundreds of centuries passin',
Till the wide ear of the wide world is deafen'd
 with wisdom!
Bellow, etc.

SOME OF THE CROWD:

Ye who have prison'd your life in the black 'n
 the gaudy red gown of the law courts,
Or think that your breast is the glittering sky
 when it's wearing the star of an order,
Ye who ply hammer 'n saw or toil on at a lathe
 in a workshop:

ALL THE CROWD TOGETHER:

Bellow good-bye to the buggerin' lot 'n come
 out
To bow down the head 'n bend down the knee
 to the bee, the bird, 'n the blossom,
Bann'ring the breast of the earth with a wonderful beauty!

(*The* BISHOP *is seen moving through the singing crowd, followed by his* SISTER. *The* BISHOP *moves about with an artificial gaiety, joining in the chorus of the song, and smiling at each person he meets as if each was an old friend, and he was a jolly good fellow. The* BISHOP'S SISTER *follows him, carrying a green parasol, closed, and showing clear signs of disapproval of the* BISHOP'S *levity. When the song has been sung the* CROWD *goes off, and we see two good-looking* NURSEMAIDS, *each with a pram in which are babies, sitting on seats at the foot of the slope. The* 1ST NURSEMAID *is reading an illustrated daily newspaper, and the* 2ND NURSEMAID *is pushing her pram to and fro, humming a tune of her own to lull the baby in it. The* BISHOP, *beaming with good humour, stands looking down the path leading towards the lake with his* SISTER *beside him.*)

BISHOP'S SISTER (*with lips tight*). This idea of getting into touch with common people is stupid, dear. They'll simply grill you with mockery. Once lose your dignity and you're done.

BISHOP (*beamingly*). Wait and see, now. I'm tired of meeting Christians with their souls dollied up for the occasion. Here's a chance of meeting the real and the raw thing, and I'm going to take it.

(*He goes over to where the* NURSEMAIDS *are sitting, and sits down on a seat beside her who is reading the paper. Deep in the pages, the* NURSEMAID *doesn't notice him. The* BISHOP'S SISTER *goes over and stands a little distance away, patiently but grimly waiting to see what may happen.*)

IST NURSEMAID (*to* 2ND NURSEMAID—*from behind her paper*). 'Ere's a picture of Ruby Pashileen end 'er lytest love—the fifth she's 'ad since she went on the films.

2ND NURSEMAID. Fancy that now! One for every dy of the week, en two for Sundyes. I shouldn't like to be going the saucy pice like that, would you, Greeta?

IST NURSEMAID. I dare sye it 'as its bright side.

2ND NURSEMAID (*trenchantly*). I mide a resolution, a definite resolution, long ago, that I'd never marry—never, never; but it was a silly thing to do, for, one dye, you might fairly meet a man you'd like, en then you'd succumb, simply succumb. But I'd never let myself be a man's——

1ST NURSEMAID (*determinedly*). Oh, Gord, no!

2ND NURSEMAID. Lots of styge lydies carry on, you know, en get gorgeous gifts for it.

1ST NURSEMAID. 'Orrible, 'orrible; one thing I'll sy, no man'll ever be able to bribe me, never, never.

(*The* BISHOP *gives a dry and embarrassed cough.*)

BISHOP'S SISTER (*putting up her parasol with a snap, and looking into the distance*). It's very hot here, Gilbert; let's seek out a shadier spot.

2ND NURSEMAID (*pushing the pram to and fro*). Must 'ave nerve, I will sy. Fancy just for a fur coat, or a bricelet 'ot with jewels, to stand in a man's room, 'is 'ands 'urrying off your silken flimsies till you stand cool en nyked in front of 'is nibs!

1ST NURSEMAID. A predicament too terrible for words.

2ND NURSEMAID. An' the agonies I go through when I'm on a chairoplane en my skirts begin to swing out in the wind!

(*The* BISHOP *gives a violent cough which attracts the attention of the* 1ST NURSEMAID, *who turns to look and sees that a clergyman's sitting beside her. An embarrassed look comes on to her face, and she gives an hysterical giggle, which she immediately checks with a hasty cough.*)

2ND NURSEMAID. Sime 'ere—agonies too terrible for words!

(*The* 1ST NURSEMAID *gives a suppressed giggle, and violently nudges her companion. The* 2ND NURSEMAID *turns her head inquiringly and sees the* BISHOP. *She immediately becomes interested with the condition of the clothes covering the child in her pram, fiddling with them, and smoothing them out.*)

BISHOP'S SISTER (*to* BISHOP). Shall we go somewhere and read a little of Tennyson?

BISHOP (*patting her arm encouragingly*). Mustn't tremble, dear, mustn't tremble. Must stiffen yourself before life in the raw. (*Bending towards a pram*) How does the little baby like her pretty nurse? Eh? Chuck, chuck, chuck!

(*The* 1ST NURSEMAID *gives a half suppressed hysterical giggle.*)

2ND NURSEMAID (*to her companion*). Shall we go, Greeta? (*She puts up the hood, and sticks her head in under it, arranging things.*)

BISHOP (*leaning over the pram so that his head is near that of the* 2ND NURSEMAID). In that day of the second coming, the leopard, the lamb, and the lion shall lie down together, and a little child shall lead them. (*To the* 2ND NURSEMAID) Snug and warm in its little nest! Oh!

(*While drawing out his head it comes into collision with the head of the* NURSEMAID. *The* 1ST NURSEMAID *giggles, coughs, then giggles again. The* BISHOP'S SISTER *looks on grimly.*)

2ND NURSEMAID (*to* 1ST NURSEMAID—*giving a giggle herself*). Wot'r you larfing at, Greeta? You are rude, I must sye.

(*The* NURSEMAIDS *prepare to go, striving to keep a giggling mood under control.*)

BISHOP (*speaking towards the kids in the prams—feelingly*). I must bless the little ones before they go. (*He stretches a hand over the prams, two fingers extended in blessing.*) May God keep these little ones from the evil that is in the world: May a gleam from the light of His holy countenance go before them all the days of their life: till they come to the grave as ripe corn reaped in due season!

(*As he is speaking the* 2ND NURSEMAID *hurries off pushing her pram, and giggling as she goes. The* 1ST NURSEMAID, *just as eager to get away, doesn't wait for the end of the blessing, but follows her companion, pushing her pram over the* BISHOP'S *toes and almost knocking him over. The* BISHOP *sits down on the seat again, embarrassed, but with his lips tight in determination. There is a pause.*)

BISHOP'S SISTER (*in a distressed voice*). There you are, you see. I told you what would happen. Can't you listen to me, Gilbert? You see what they are like now. Don't you realise that all this is very humiliating to your sister?

BISHOP (*with grim dignity*). Through His unworthy servant, in face of the laughter of fools, God has blessed the little ones; yea, and they shall be blessed.

(*A Pause.*)

BISHOP'S SISTER. Shall we go somewhere, dear, and read a little of Tennyson?

BISHOP (*snappily*). Oh, damn old Tennyson!

(*The* BISHOP'S SISTER *stares for a few moments at the* BISHOP. *As she is staring, the* TWO CHAIR ATTENDANTS, *lamer than ever, and looking older, enter, mouch limpingly over to a bench at the foot of the slope to the left, and sit down wearily. They no longer wear their khaki overalls or peaked caps.*

They sit, one at each end of the seat, so that they can recline against the arms of the bench.)

OLDER ATTENDANT (*as they come in*). Too slow! Why there's years of 'opping abaht in us still. 'Ad 'is own fyvourites f'r the job, 'e 'ad, Godfrey. En' when I thinks of us, en' when I thinks of 'er!

YOUNGER ATTENDANT. Forgit it, forgit it, Bysil.

(*They sit down and cuddle themselves up for a drowse on the bench.*)

BISHOP'S SISTER. If you insist on this sort of thing, Gilbert, I shall go over to the seat under the oak tree near the bandstand. You'll find me there, if you want me.

BISHOP (*doggedly*). I'm going to see this thing through.

(*The* BISHOP'S SISTER *goes up the centre path, and goes out over the slope. The* BISHOP *sits on grimly, with an eye on the* ATTENDANTS.)

YOUNGER ATTENDANT (*half asleep*). Carn't git it aht of me brine. When I thinks of us, en' then when I thinks of 'er!

OLDER ATTENDANT (*half asleep*). Doesn't bear thinking of, I thinks.

YOUNGER ATTENDANT (*with sleepy bitterness*).

Daughtaw of a lyebor leader. 'Er first dawnce in 'er fatheh's 'ouse. Two ushers in blue velvet coats en' yellow velvet britches, with white styeves to guide the visitors in.

OLDER ATTENDANT (*sleepily*). Forgit it, Godfrey; not good to dwell on it, en' us aht of a job.

YOUNGER ATTENDANT (*with sleepy bitterness*). In en emerald green gown, costing 'undreds, with glittering bands of jewel green en sapphire blue crossing over 'er byre back. Oh, when I thinks of us, en' then, when I thinks of 'er!

OLDER ATTENDANT (*sinking to slumber*). Forgit the blue en' yellow velvet, the jewel green en' sapphire blue on the byre back, en' ransom 'unger with a little sleep.

(*The* BISHOP *stiffens himself out of his gloom. He gives a self-encouraging cough. He stands up, and looks towards the* TWO ATTENDANTS *half asleep on the bench. He gives himself a little shake, smiles, and coughs gently. Then, after a moment's hesitation, he goes briskly over to the bench, and breezily sits down between them. The* TWO MEN *half open their eyes, and look at him.*)

BISHOP (*gustily to the* TWO MEN, *as he sits down between them*). Morning, men. Having a little nap in the sun, eh? Good men, good men.

OLDER ATTENDANT (*with a poor attempt at brightness*). Yessir. Me en' Godfrey's aht of werk, en' the 'eat myde us a bit 'eavy.

BISHOP (*motioning towards the hollyhocks*). Damn fine flowers, aren't they?

OLDER ATTENDANT (*not looking at the flowers*). Yessir—damn fine. Nice thing to see, sir, a clergyman merry en' bright, en' ready to tork to 'umble men, like us,—isn't it Godfrey?

(*The birds sing brightly.*)

YOUNGER ATTENDANT (*with dignity*). I concur with thet.

BISHOP (*gustily*). Oh, the Church isn't the solemn thing people think. She can laugh, sing, and skip at a suitable time, at a suitable time.

OLDER ATTENDANT (*warily watching the* BISHOP). I alwyes said the clergy were 'ooman —didn't I, Godfrey?

YOUNGER ATTENDANT. Often en' often, ri' enough.

OLDER ATTENDANT. We're too 'ard up to be merry, 'm aht of werk; nothing to eat, en' nowhere to go. A five shilling piece, now, would werk a miracle, sir—wouldn't it, Godfrey?

YOUNGER ATTENDANT. I must sye I concur with thet.

(*A stony look comes on the* BISHOP'S *face, and he looks silently in front of him. A short pause.*)

OLDER ATTENDANT (*almost tearfully*). Or even a two shilling piece each, would give me en' Godfrey a dandy glimpse of heaven; wouldn't it, Godfrey?

YOUNGER ATTENDANT. The reverend gentleman 'as a wide 'eart, I'd sye.

BISHOP (*with tightened lips*). I never do that sort of thing. I never give charity without careful investigation.

(*The* TWO ATTENDANTS *lean back on the bench, and there is a rather long pause. The birds stop singing.*)

OLDER ATTENDANT (*with sudden vehemence*). En' wot the 'ell, then, didja want to plank yourself dahn between where two poor men were trying to get a spot of slumber?

(*The* BISHOP *sits silent, still upright and tight-lipped, staring in front of him.*)

(*With slow and grumbling bitterness*) 'Undreds en' 'undreds of seats, scattered everywhere, crying aht for arses, en' along comes a person 'oo crushes 'imself in where two men is trying to dope 'unger en' unemployment with a little sleep!

YOUNGER ATTENDANT (*mutteringly*). Flopping dahn with mischievous 'ilarity were 'e warn't wanted.

OLDER ATTENDANT (*decisively*). Sing en' 'op en' skip—well, I knows one as 'opes the church'll 'op up en' skip off somewhere else.

YOUNGER ATTENDANT (*emphatically*). I concur with thet!

OLDER ATTENDANT. En' these are the sort of sacerdotal nippies running rahnd trying to get us to torture ourselves with pryer en' penitence, en' lowering the stattus of the rice!

YOUNGER ATTENDANT. Miking religion a larfing-stock, they are.

(*The* BISHOP *takes a book out of his side pocket, and with a stubborn look on his face, opens it and starts to read.*)

OLDER ATTENDANT. Oh, we're a going to stye on en' read, are we? Well, if I was sitting on a bench where I knew I warn't wanted, en' got a 'int to go, I'd push off, wouldn't you, Godfrey?

YOUNGER ATTENDANT. Quick.

BISHOP (*with dignified determination*). I choose this place in which to rest, and I shall go when I think it dignified to do so.

OLDER ATTENDANT. We 'as the first clime to the plice, en' we warnt to tork private.

(*The* BISHOP *takes no notice, but goes on reading his book.*

A pause.)

YOUNGER ATTENDANT (*to* OLDER ATTENDANT). Oh, look at the little peach what's coming along, Bysil.

(*The* YOUNG WHORE *comes in. She is paler looking than before, and a few lines are visible under her eyes. She is walking jauntily along, hesitates a moment when she sees the* BISHOP, *then, after glancing at the* TWO MEN *beside the* BISHOP, *she goes on and out again.*)

OLDER ATTENDANT (*knowingly—to* YOUNGER ATTENDANT). See 'is nibs tiking en eyeful over the top of the book of wot was passing.

(*The* BISHOP *remains silent and doggedly goes on with his reading.*

The OLDER ATTENDANT *leans over the back of the bench to talk to his companion, who leans back to listen, while the* BISHOP *leans forward, still reading his book, to avoid their touch.*)

(*In a hoarse whisper*) Know wot I'd like to do, honest? Gambol a gime with en 'eifer in front of a clergyman, strite, I would. Show 'im a little of the gaiety of life, strite, I would!

(*The birds on the branches twitter more loudly than ever.*)

YOUNGER ATTENDANT. Don't know as it would shock 'em a lot, Bysil; I'd bet they 'as their 'ectic moments on the sly.

OLDER ATTENDANT (*getting up from the seat in his zeal*). You bet they 'as. Wot do they do in their palaces when the lamps is lighted en' the blinds is drawn? We eats, they eats; we drinks, they drinks; we sleeps, they sleeps; but wot's done in the empty spices of the night time? Wot do they do in their palaces when the lamps is lighted en' the blinds is drawn?

(*The* YOUNG WHORE *enters and, after a glance towards the* BISHOP, *sits down on a seat directly opposite, takes out mirror and puff from her handbag, and gives her face a few deft touches.*)

YOUNGER ATTENDANT (*rising from his seat and poking the* OLDER ATTENDANT *in the side, with a sly glance towards the* YOUNG WHORE). 'Owidge you like to tuck 'er up et night, Bysil?

(*Suddenly in the distance is heard the roll on a muffled drum, and the mournful notes of the chant of the* DOWN-AND-OUTS. *The birds cease their singing; the scene seems to grow dark, and the air chilly. The* TWO CHAIR ATTENDANTS *stiffen, and fright comes over their faces. The* YOUNG WHORE *half rises from her seat, turns pale, and leans a hand on the back of the seat.*)

DOWN-AND-OUTS (*chanting in the distance*):

Life has pass'd us by to the loud roll of her drum,
With her waving flags of yellow and green held high,
All starr'd with the golden, flaming names of her most mighty children.

(*The chant fades away.*

The CHAIR ATTENDANTS *slouch out, bent-backed and silent, one to the right and the other to the left, as the chant fades. The* YOUNG WHORE *sinks down slowly on to the seat, frightened and shivering. The scene brightens, and the birds sing a little. There is a pause. The* YOUNG WHORE *is sitting, sad and thoughtful, opposite the* BISHOP. *She is very attractive-looking, sitting there in her tailor-made coat and skirt, and her bright helmet hat. Her slim legs, looking slimmer in their elegant silk stockings, are for all to see from the knees down. The* BISHOP *suddenly sighs, closes the book he has been reading, puts it in his pocket and, turning a little round, sees the* YOUNG WHORE. *He looks at her pretty face, thoughtfully bent towards the ground, at her neatly dressed body, and, finally, his eyes linger a little over the slim legs visible from the knees down. An old interest seems to stir in him as he looks at her. Ashamed, he turns his head away for a few moments. He looks at her again, first at her face, then at her body, and then, more consciously, at her legs. He turns his gaze away again, and moves uneasily in his seat, lets his head sink forward till his chin rests on his breast. He lifts his head and looks at her; she turns at the same time, and they stare at each other for a moment; then the* BISHOP'S *head sinks down on his breast again.*

Suddenly the YOUNG WHORE *rises swiftly, as if she had come to a sudden resolution, hurries to where the* BISHOP *is, sits down on the bench beside him, and, catching his arm, speaks to him imploringly.*)

YOUNG WHORE (*appealingly*). I want you to help me. You are near to God, but I am out of reach.

BISHOP (*frightened*). Oh, my child, I'm afraid I can help only those whom I know.

YOUNG WHORE. Listen to me, listen to me, first. My heart is bad, and doctors say that death may seize me at any moment, and take me out of life. There's a young man who loves me, and is going to marry me, but I want you to come with me to see him, and make him marry me at once.

BISHOP (*bewildered*). But I know nothing about you or about him.

YOUNG WHORE. You will, please, you must; you are a man after God's own heart—you'll help a young girl whose one chance is help at once.

BISHOP (*frightened to be talking to the girl—looking round him nervously*). Why do you run to the priest for help only when you begin to feel the terrible consequences of your shame?

YOUNG WHORE (*irritated at the* BISHOP'S *thought*). Oh, I'm not going to have a kid, man, if that's what you mean. Nothing like that for me yet, thank you! It's because I'd love to have one that I came to you;—to save me from falling into the condition that could never give me one.

BISHOP. But you can't discuss such things with a man and a perfect stranger, girl.

YOUNG WHORE. You're neither a man nor a stranger: you are a priest of the most high God.

BISHOP (*frightened and petulant*). Oh, be sensible, girl! Go and talk of these things with your father and mother.

YOUNG WHORE (*bitterly*). I never knew my father, and my mother drinks and hates me.

BISHOP (*with ostentatious indignation*). You mustn't talk like that about your mother. Whatever she may be, she should be sacred to you.

YOUNG WHORE (*with scorn*). Oh, sacred to me! A mother can be sacred only when she makes herself sacred to her children;—can't you understand that, man?

BISHOP (*coldly*). I have no help to offer you, and I must ask you to go away, please.

YOUNG WHORE (*impulsively sitting down beside the* BISHOP). Do listen to me, please do, Lord Bishop. I've seen you talking and laughing with common people, and it gave me heart to speak to you.

BISHOP (*in his best manner, putting his hand on her knee, and patting it*). Go and live with your mother and show her you realise what a mother really is. Work steadily, cultivate thrifty habits, and in a few years' time you'll be able to face marriage far more brightly and firmly than you could possibly face it now.

YOUNG WHORE (*trembling and agitated, pushing his hand from her knee*). Oh, piping out of you the same old rot that I've heard a thousand times—mother, work, and thrift! (*Indignantly*) If you knew what a rip she was, I wonder if you'd like to live with her? I wonder, if you were a girl, and good-looking, would you bray about the happiness of work? (*Raising her voice a little*) Do you know why I had to fly out of the two last jobs I was in, had to—d'ye hear—had to fly out of them?

BISHOP (*taking a book from his pocket and beginning to read—coldly*). I do not want to know the reason.

YOUNG WHORE (*vehemently*). Because I wouldn't let the manager see how I looked with nothing on. Oh, you hide behind your book when facts frighten you. There's many an old graven image has made a girl dance out of her job and chance the streets, sooner than strip herself for his benefit, with nine hours a day and three pounds a week added on to the pleasure.

BISHOP (*from behind his book*). You mustn't annoy me in this way. Please leave me in peace.

YOUNG WHORE (*with great vehemence*). It's the truth. Can't you put your book down for a second and listen? (*She pushes the book aside.*) Come with me to the shop and I'll bring you face to face with him.

(*The* TWO NURSEMAIDS *come in pushing their prams; they both look at the* BISHOP *and the* YOUNG WHORE. *The* 1ST NURSEMAID *giggles as she goes by.*)

2ND NURSEMAID (*to her companion—giggling herself as they go out*). Greeta, you are rude I must sye!

BISHOP (*nervous at the notice taken—looking over the top of his book*). Will you be good enough to go away, please?

YOUNG WHORE (*imploringly*). Please listen to me. Are you afraid to find a lie in what you think to be the truth, or the truth in what you think to be a lie? Come and tell the manager you're my friend, and make him give me back the job I had to leave. Oh, do, do, please!

(*The* BISHOP *looks around him in nervous agitation and sees the* YOUNG MAN IN PLUS-FOURS *looking down at them from the slope above, who hurries off when the* BISHOP *sees him.*)

(*After a pause*) Won't you help me?

BISHOP (*in cold and final tones*). No.

(*A pause.*)

YOUNG WHORE (*with quiet bitterness*). I suppose you'd have helped me had I let you go on handling my knee.

BISHOP (*in cold and tense tones to the* YOUNG WHORE). If you don't go away at once I'll have you handed over to the police for annoying me!

(*The* YOUNG WHORE *sits silent and shocked for a few moments, looking fixedly at the* BISHOP.)

YOUNG WHORE (*mockingly*). Oh, hand me over to a policeman, would you? I see. Easy way of getting over a difficulty by handing it over to a policeman. Get back, get back, please; gangway, gangway, there. Policemen making a gangway for Jesus Christ. (*She stands up.*)

(*The* BISHOP *stiffens himself behind his book.*)

(*With intense scorn and bitterness*) You and your goodness are no use to God. If Christ came again, He'd have to call, not the sinners, but the righteous to repentance. Go out into the sun and pick the yellow primroses! Take your elegant and perfum'd soul out of the stress, and stain, the horrid cries, the noisy laugh of life, an' go out into the sun, an' pick the yellow primroses! When you go to where your God is throned, tell the gaping saints you never soiled a hand in Jesu's service. Tell them a pretty little whore, well on her way to hell, once tempted you to help her; but you saved yourself by the calm and cunning of a holy mind, an' went out into the sun to pick the yellow primroses, leaving her, sin-soddened, in the strain, the stain, the horrid cries, an' the noisy laugh of life. Tell them you were ever calm before the agony in other faces, an', an' the tip of your finger never touched a brow beaded with a bloody sweat!

> (*The horrified* BISHOP *suddenly closes his book, and rises from his seat to go away, but the* YOUNG WHORE *with a vigorous push from her hand, sends him sitting down in the seat again.*)

YOUNG WHORE (*passionately, thrusting her face close to the* BISHOP'S). A tired Christ would be afraid to lean on your arm. Your Christ wears a bowler hat, carries a cane, twiddles his lavender gloves, an' sends out gilt-edged cards of thanks to callers. Out with you, you old shivering sham, an' go away into the sun to pick the yellow primroses!

> (*As the* YOUNG WHORE *is speaking her last few sentences the* OLD WOMAN

enters. She is pale and haggard, and vicious lines harden the look of her mouth. Her hair is white, but her black eyes are still undimmed by age. Her thin body is still upright, showing that in her youth she was slim and vigorous, and her face still shelters traces of what were once very good looks. Her boots, though polished, are old and broken, and everything about her, though old and patched and shabby, is clean and neat. Constant, quiet drinking has made her a little incoherent in her thoughts. In one hand she carries a small wreath of red poppies and laurel leaves, which has a bunch of violets where the wreath is tied together by a bow of black ribbon. She has heard the voice of the YOUNG WHORE, *and comes down to where the girl is speaking, gripping her roughly by the arm as the* YOUNG WHORE *is about to go away from the* BISHOP.)

OLD WOMAN (*to the* YOUNG WHORE). Putting yourself again on the market for men, are you? Piling up money, and not a penny nor the thought of a penny for your lonely and suffering mother. (*As the* YOUNG WHORE *tries to free herself*) No use you trying to get away. (*She drops the wreath on the ground, and holds the girl tighter.*) I have you and I hold you till I get a little to help me on in life for a week or two!

YOUNG WHORE (*morosely*). I haven't any money, and, even if I had, I wouldn't part with a penny to you, for all you want it for is drink.

OLD WOMAN (*furiously*). Drink! Hear that now! Is it any wonder God has given her a heart that may go phut any minute? (*Over to the* BISHOP) Hear what she said, you?—that I want the money for drink!

YOUNG WHORE (*with a frightened, scornful laugh*). Let me go, will you? If my heart does go phut, I'll go game, see? Pass out dancing, see?

(*The* OLD WOMAN *claws at the girl's hat, pulls it off her head, and flings it on the ground, then tugs savagely at the girl's coat.*)

OLD WOMAN (*wildly*). Want the money for drink, do I? I'll tear every stitch on you into ribbons!

YOUNG WHORE (*imploringly*). Please, please, mother, don't ruin the few decent little things I have to wear!

(*The* BISHOP *gets up from his seat, goes*

over to the struggling women, and tries to separate them.)

BISHOP (*trying to restore peace*). For shame, for shame! Mother and daughter,—for shame, for shame!

(*As soon as she hears the* BISHOP'S *voice, the* OLD WOMAN *releases her hold on the girl, and stares at the* BISHOP. *The* YOUNG WHORE, *excited and exhausted, sinks into a seat a little distance away. The* BISHOP *returns the* OLD WOMAN'S *look for a moment, and then rather hastily returns to his seat and resumes the reading of his book The* OLD WOMAN'S *eyes follow the* BISHOP *and, after a moment's hesitation, she comes up close to him.*)

OLD WOMAN (*looking fixedly at the* BISHOP—*murmuringly*). Your voice has a strange echo in it. Behind that wizened face is hidden a look of the first young man who conquered me on a Sunday night, after the ora pro nobis people had pulled down their blinds and were slinking into sleep. There under a yellow moon, among the shadows by a grove of birch trees, on a bed of flattened bluebells, one of the prettiest fillies that ever wore a skirt was jockeyed into sin, and out of the rapture and the risk came a girl who puts her clothes on to take them off again for any man who pays her well enough to take the trouble. (*Suddenly*) Is your name Gilbert?

BISHOP (*over the top of his book—looking disturbed and uneasy*). Go away, you wretched and forgotten creature!

OLD WOMAN (*still staring at him—murmuringly*). I'm not much to look at now, but the man who first got the better of me's a big jack-a-dandy in the church now, for I saw him once in a holy procession, helping to sing a canticle, with a purple cape hanging on his shoulders. (*Suddenly pushing the* BISHOP'S *book aside*) Eh, you, is your name Gilbert?

BISHOP (*roughly*). Get away, get away, woman. My name's not Gilbert; get away, I tell you!

(*The* OLD WOMAN *goes over to the* YOUNG WHORE *limply sitting on a seat. The* BISHOP *leans forward with his elbows on his knees and his head in his hands.*)

OLD WOMAN (*to the* YOUNG WHORE*—whiningly*). Why don't you try to be decent to your poor mother? She won't trouble you for long. I feel a few more months'll see the end of me.

YOUNG WHORE (*savagely*). I'd dance and sing if I thought you'd die in an hour!

OLD WOMAN (*wildly*). You'd dance and sing if I died in an hour? Hear that, now? Dance and sing! How can God listen to such a saying and not strike you dead? (*Over to the* BISHOP) Didja hear what she said?—dance and sing if I died in an hour? Come over and bruise her hopes with a grim curse from God.

BISHOP (*his hands covering his face*). Oh, hush, hush, woman; hush and go home.

OLD WOMAN (*wrathful at the* BISHOP'S *indifference*). Hush, hush, and go home you! Hear what she said to me, said to her mother? Dance if I died in an hour, and you take her part. You ought to be driven helter-skelter out of everything holy. Hush you, and go home, with your ora pro pugeree mugeree rigmarolum!

(*The* DREAMER *appears on the slope above and looks on at those below.*)

(*Turning violently on the* YOUNG WHORE) In league with you, is he? (*She seizes hold of the* YOUNG WHORE *and shakes her violently*) Dance if I was dead to-day, or died to-morrow, would you?

YOUNG WHORE (*terrified*). Mother, mind; don't—I didn't mean anything!

OLD WOMAN (*shaking her more violently still*). I think of nothing but drink, do I not?

YOUNG WHORE (*hysterically*). My heart, my heart—you'll be the death of me.

OLD WOMAN (*fiercely flinging her back so that the* YOUNG WHORE *falls to the ground on her knees*). I'll teach you a little of the duty a daughter owes to her mother!

(*She raises her arm to strike the* YOUNG WHORE, *but the* DREAMER, *who has come close, seizes her, and prevents the arm from falling. The* BISHOP *has risen, frightened, makes a step forward to stop the row, but stops in hesitation.*)

DREAMER (*gently shaking the* OLD WOMAN). Now then, now then, what's this?

(*The* YOUNG WHORE *pulls herself up on a seat, her heart beating rapidly, so that she finds it difficult to breathe. She is very frightened, and a little hysterical.*)

YOUNG WHORE (*panting and hysterical*). Get her away; send her away, for God's sake!

DREAMER (*coaxingly, but firmly pushing the* OLD WOMAN *out*). Go on away, old woman. Better go home.

OLD WOMAN (*murmuringly, as she goes out*). No pity in the young: only waiting for time to hustle us off. (*Turns her head back to look at the* YOUNG WHORE) Making money out of woman's gift to man. I never did that. What I did, I did for the love of the thing; did it and was done with it, till it had to be done again. (*She gently brushes the laurel wreath which she has picked up, with her hand.*) The bad present, and the good absent; the shame living, and the pride buried; gone from my grasp and my sight in the smoke and flame of the war. O Jesus, is there no rest to be found anywhere!

(*The* OLD WOMAN *goes out, and the* DREAMER, *hurrying back to the* YOUNG WHORE, *sees the* BISHOP *beckoning to him, and he goes over to him.*)

BISHOP (*anxiously*). Think she'll be all right?

DREAMER. Yes, she'll be all right again in a second.

BISHOP (*handing the* DREAMER *two pound notes*). Give her these; she may need them. Don't say I gave them,—just slip them into her bag when you get a chance; and keep an eye on her till she has recovered, will you?

DREAMER. Sure.

BISHOP. Thanks.

(*The* BISHOP *goes up centre path to the slope, looking back anxiously at the* YOUNG WHORE; *he crosses the slope, and gives another glance as he goes out. The* DREAMER *returns to the* YOUNG WHORE.)

DREAMER (*to the* YOUNG WHORE). Feeling a little better now?

YOUNG WHORE (*still panting a little*). Bit better now. It's my heart—goes curious now when anything happens. Please sit down beside me for a minute or two.

DREAMER. For a year and a day, if you like.

(*He sits beside her and takes her hand in his and strokes it.*)

YOUNG WHORE (*bitterly*). I'll go off in one of these attacks yet. Nice thing to have for a mother, isn't she? I love the dear silver that shines in her hair! Feeling better, now, anyhow. (*Slyly*) How do you like the hand?

DREAMER. Lovely—like a blue-veined, pink-tipp'd lily.

YOUNG WHORE (*taking her hand away*). Well, let it go for a minute, till I straighten myself up a little.

(*She arranges her hat, smoothes the folds of her skirt, gives a few touches to her blouse, and sits down again.*)

I'm a little more presentable now.

DREAMER (*moving a hand semi-circularly over her breasts*). There's a wrinkle or two in your blouse still.

YOUNG WHORE (*taking his hand away*). Dad's spoken about you. Not the real dad,—never saw my real father—The Atheist, you know: calls you a poet. How do you live?

DREAMER (*mockingly*). Hold a meeting here every night, and make a collection sufficient to keep the bank from failing; and sell an odd story. But oughtn't you to get home and have a rest? I'll see you safe there.

YOUNG WHORE (*slyly*). Tuck me up and sing me to sleep with one of your songs.

DREAMER (*eagerly*). I'd love to. He brought me home to his house of wine, and his banner over me was love. (*Getting up, and catching her arm*) Come on, dear, come on.

YOUNG WHORE (*pulling her arm free and speaking a little sharply*). Not so quick, please. Men are always ready to rush a pretty woman into bed looking for joy and behold trouble. (*A pause.*) Supposing I go and give, what do I get?

DREAMER. I'll pay your merry kindness with a song.

YOUNG WHORE (*scornfully*). A song! A puff of scented air! You're out on the hunt for bargains, young man. Goods reduced to the lowest possible figure;—actually given away. Go with a priest for a prayer, and with a poet for a song! It's hardly likely, as the soldier said to the lady.

DREAMER (*sitting down beside her, and looking*

earnestly into her face). My dear young girl, queens most lovely have been snared in the golden meshes of a poet's song.

YOUNG WHORE (*good-humouredly*). Well, let's see if one of yours can snare the heart of a pretty little whore.

DREAMER. Wait till we get to your flat so that I can kiss you between the verses.

YOUNG WHORE. Oh, you're travelling quick along your own little road, young singer. Sing it now or sing it never.

DREAMER (*resignedly*). Oh, alright, then. We'll call it by your name—what is it?

YOUNG WHORE. Just Jannice.

DREAMER. What a pretty name! Well, we'll call the song, just *Jannice*. (*He gives a shy little cough and sings*—)

Her legs are as pliant and slim
As fresh, golden branches of willow;
I see lustre of love on each limb,
Looking down from the heights of a pillow!
Looking down from the heights of a pillow!

Tossed by a soft breeze in the Spring,
The blooms of an apple tree billow;
And her breasts are as lovely to me,
Looking down from the heights of a pillow,
Looking down from the heights of a pillow!

Gay, white apple blossoms her breast,
Her legs golden branches of willow;
I'd enjoy for a year and a day,
Looking down from the heights of a pillow,
Looking down from the heights of a pillow!

(*After a pause—expectantly*). Well?

YOUNG WHORE (*with a touch of scorn in her voice*). I'm afraid you'll have to give me a greater encouragement than a song to get me to go with you. (*With a laugh*) Go to bed and wake up to find a song under the clock! Can't you add something to the song, dear?

(*A pause. The* BISHOP *comes up the path from the lake, starts to go over to them, thinks better of it, and remains away at the back. The* YOUNG MAN IN PLUS-FOURS *comes in from the left, passes by the* YOUNG WHORE *and the* DREAMER, *glances at the girl as he passes, and sits down some distance away so as to face towards the girl. She returns his glances, and moves on her seat so as to bring her legs into view of the* YOUNG MAN IN PLUS-FOURS. *A band in the distance begins to play the Blue Danube Waltz. The* GARDENER *appears on the slope, comes down, and arranges the hollyhocks, watching the* YOUNG WHORE *as he does so.)*

DREAMER (*hesitatingly*). I could manage a pound.

YOUNG WHORE. That's a little better. Let's see how it looks, while we listen to the band playing the Blue Danube Waltz.

(*The* DREAMER *takes a note from his pocket, gives it to her, and she puts it in her bag, as she hums the tune of the waltz the band is playing. The* YOUNG MAN IN PLUS-FOURS *gets up from his seat, goes up centre path towards the slope, giving the* YOUNG WHORE *an inviting glance as he passes, and stands at the right corner of the slope. The* YOUNG WHORE *stands up.*)

YOUNG WHORE (*to the* DREAMER). I must be off; see you some other time. Go and listen to the band. Good-bye, and thanks.

DREAMER (*astonished*). Why, amn't I going with you?

YOUNG WHORE (*mockingly*). Not this time, dear. The exchange isn't good enough.

(*She waltzes up the centre path, the* DREAMER *gaping after her.*)

DREAMER (*bitterly*). A thief, be God, as well as a whore!

(*The* BISHOP *watches her, takes a step towards her, then stops where he is. The* YOUNG MAN IN PLUS-FOURS, *seeing her coming to him, goes slowly out.*)

GARDENER (*appealingly to the* YOUNG WHORE *as she goes by him*). Jannice, don't go with him! (*As she dances on.*) Jannice!

(*The* YOUNG WHORE *dances on out after the* YOUNG MAN IN PLUS-FOURS.)

BISHOP (*imploringly as she goes out*). Jannice!

The BISHOP *sits down on a seat, and buries his face in his hands. The music grows louder, and seems to mock the three men as—*

THE GATES CLOSE

SCENE III

An Autumn Evening.

The same as the preceding one; but the colours of the sky have changed to yellow, with a faint orange glow in the centre, deepening into a melancholy purple border wherever the trees and shrubbery do not hide the horizon. The leaves on the trees have turned to various shades of red, bronze, or golden yellow, and now and again a number of them fall fluttering to the ground. At odd intervals are still heard the notes of the birds and the cries of the waterfowl. Where the dahlias were there is a clump of tall, gaunt sunflowers, whose conventionalised blossoms look like huge golden discs writhing with pain. The figure of the steel-hatted soldier is shot with the orange-glow from the sky. The air is heavy with the breath of life, which has panted on to its fullest vigour, and is now beginning to decay and die. The sails of the little boats as they pass by are in the shadow, and are sometimes purple and sometimes black, and seem to be huge beetles moving slowly over the ripple-free water.

The TWO CHAIR ATTENDANTS, *deprived of their jobs, are lying half asleep on benches, one to the right, and the other to the left. They are in the semi-final state of decay, with clothes tattered and faces worn, haggard and anxious. The* YOUNG MAN IN PLUS-FOURS, *hatless, is standing on the top of the slope, with a slender white wand in his hand. He is directing the community singing of a crowd gathered below him, which cannot be seen. As the Scene opens he is wiping sweat from his brow. As he does so the* SCARLET WOMAN *passes by him over the slope, giving him the customary inviting glance as she goes by. He hastily returns the handkerchief to his pocket, and stretches out his wand as an indication to the crowd below to get ready.*

YOUNG MAN IN PLUS-FOURS (*down to the* CROWD *below. He is facing away from the front*). Quicker this time, please. Now!

(CROWD *below singing.*)

CROWD:

Land of hope and glory, mother of the free,
How can we extol thee, who were born of thee?

Wider still and wider let thy boundary be:
God, who made thee mighty, make thee mightier still,
God, who made thee mighty, make thee mightier still.

(*While the crowd are singing, the* YOUNG MAN IN PLUS-FOURS *turns his head and stretches his neck to watch where the* SCARLET WOMAN *is going. When the song has ended on a long-drawn-out note, the* YOUNG MAN IN PLUS-FOURS *puts the wand in his pocket, picks up his cap from the ground, and hurries out after the* SCARLET WOMAN. *The singing wakes the* TWO ATTENDANTS, *who listen with sleepy indignation.*)

OLDER ATTENDANT (*in a vicious grumble*). Won't let a man nestle dahn nowhere in peace!

(*A pause.*)

OLDER ATTENDANT (*drowsily*). Wot you said abaht the pahnd, Godfrey, won't 'old, won't 'old. I still thinks we lost our 'eads when we un'ooked the pahnd from the gold stennerd. Tride looks a 'ead, en' says the pahnd'll rise; but the pahnd goes dahn, en' tride's up the pole. Tride looks a 'ead agine, en' says the pahnd'll go dahn; but the pahnd goes up, en' tride's a 'anging in the ire; Oh, it was a giddy thing to go off sterling!

YOUNGER ATTENDANT (*drowsily*). Give the British pahnd a charnce in the world's market, I says. Why when it was on the stennerd, we was losing our gold in shiploads—no, let the British pahnd tike its charnce in the world's market, I says!

OLDER ATTENDANT (*sinking into sleep*). Shiploads of our gold going orf, en' we 'aven't as much as id buy a blarsted bun!

(*The* TWO NURSEMAIDS *enter pushing their prams; on one of the prams is a gramophone. The* 1ST NURSEMAID *is dressed in blouse and shorts, and the* BOY *follows at her heels. The* NURSEMAIDS *look furtively behind them as they come in. The* TWO ATTENDANTS *are now almost asleep, each on his own bench.*)

1ST NURSEMAID (*dressed in shorts*). Don't look rahnd, don't look rahnd.

2ND NURSEMAID. Oh, I'd try en' forgive 'im, even if 'e was to blime. You never knows wot a quarrel'll lead to—may mean a parting forever.

YOUNG BOY (*to* 1ST NURSEMAID). What was the man doing, Nannie, waving the white wand?

1ST NURSEMAID (*to* BOY). Conductin' the

community singing, dear. (*To* 2ND NURSEMAID) No, I'm determined to be adamant. His sister! I seen the pire of them among the bushes, en' 'e tuckin' 'er into 'im.

BOY. What's community singing, Nannie?

1ST NURSEMAID (*to the* BOY). Community singing's just community singing, dear. (*To* 2ND NURSEMAID) I don't allow for deception. If he wants to paride abaht with a femile, 'e can't 'ave me. When 'e knew 'ow to respect me, 'e 'ad me; when 'e doesn't, 'e 'asn't, en' I'm determined to be adamant.

2ND NURSEMAID (*in a whisper*). 'Ere 'e comes creepin' along, Greeta; Oh, 'is fice 'as altered, worn en' un'appy, like—'e is suffering, Greeta!

BOY (*to* 1ST NURSEMAID). Why's that kind of singing called community singing, Nannie?

(*The* GUARDSMAN *enters slowly, and gazes with a doleful stare at the* 1ST NURSEMAID, *who turns her back on him, busies herself with the pram, and deliberately takes no notice of him.*)

BOY (*pulling at the shorts of the* 1ST NURSEMAID). Why's community singing called community singing, Nannie?

1ST NURSEMAID (*irritably to the* BOY). Don't do that—you'll pull them off me!

(*The* GUARDSMAN *passes by the* NURSEMAIDS, *turns and looks back pitifully and pleadingly at the* 1ST NURSEMAID, *who persists in taking no notice of him; he then goes slowly out.*)

2ND NURSEMAID (*pityingly*). I felt for 'im when I seen the sorrowful look in his eyes, Greeta; you are 'ard.

BOY (*to* 1ST NURSEMAID). Why's community singing called community singing, Nannie?

1ST NURSEMAID (*angrily—to the* BOY). Can't you see Reeta an' me's talkin' important? Enother squeak from you, en' you'll hear no gramophone record this evenin'.

2ND NURSEMAID (*to the* BOY). You mustn't interrupt, Georgie, when we're torkin' serious. Community singin's the singin' of songs by the community at large.

1ST NURSEMAID (*as they move off*). No, Reeta, unless 'e writes en' apologises, unless 'e writes en' explines; unless 'e writes en' asks me to forgive 'im, 'e'll never 'andle a chance of bein' with yours truly agine!

2ND NURSEMAID (*following her out*). You are 'ard, I must sy.

BOY (*following the* NURSEMAIDS). What's a community at large, Nannie?

(*From the right and from the left, vari-*

ously, the FOREMAN, *the* MAN WITH THE STICK, *the* MAN IN THE BOWLER HAT, *a* MAN IN SHORTS, *and others, come in. Each carries a newspaper under an arm, and each carries a light, formally designed deck-chair in the right hand. They come in with stiff, conventionalised steps. They arrange the chairs, and sit down together. They take out the papers and unfold them in three or four staccato movements, and then begin to read. They hold the papers so that a page appears before each reader like a placard. On one paper is the word "Murder"; on another the word "Rape"; on another the word "Divorce"; on another the word "Racing"; on another the word "Suicide"; on another the word "Execution"; and on another the words "Great Cricketer Talks About God". After a few moments, a gramophone is heard playing "London Bridge is Falling Down". The music awakens the* TWO ATTENDANTS; *silently they take their legs off the benches, get up, and indignantly limp away to seek a more peaceful resting-place.)*

THE GRAMOPHONE:

London Bridge is falling down, falling down, falling down;
London Bridge is falling down, my fair lady.
Build it up with gold and silver, gold and silver, gold and silver;
Build it up with gold and silver, my fair lady.

(*During the singing of the second verse, the* READERS *have looked angrily over the tops of their papers towards where the gramophone is playing.*)

Gold and silver will not do, will not do, will not do;
Gold and silver will not do, my fair lady.

(*The* YOUNG WHORE *appears on the slope above and sings the last verse with the gramophone. She is still dressed in her black tailor-made suit, with its crimson crescent on the hip; and her crimson hat decorated with its black crescent. She sings in a jaunty way, for she is a little excited with wine. She comes down, moving among the* READERS, *rustling their precious papers, and disturbing their peace. The* BISHOP *enters above and watches the movements of the girl. He has aged, and the gay look he forced on to his face is gone, leaving it uneasy-looking and sadly lined. He seems restless and timid, coming down a few steps, going back and standing again to watch.)*

READERS (*singing low but steadily behind their papers*):

Gold and silver's grown a god, grown a god, grown a god;
Gold and silver's grown a god,
My fair lady!

YOUNG WHORE (*singing in reply savagely*):

Let it fall to pieces then, pieces then, pieces then;
Let it fall to pieces then,
My fair lady!

(*She surveys the* READERS *for a few moments, looking at them thoughtfully. Then she ironically lifts her hand in a gesture for silent reverence.*)

YOUNG WHORE. Hush, hush, the oblate brothers are busy reading the gospel for the day. Sucking in holy thoughts of holy wisdom. Let us pray. Oh Lucifer, Lucifer, who has caused all newspapers, stars of the morning and stars of the evening, to be written for our learning, grant that we may so read that we may always find punch in them, hot stuff in them, and sound tips in them, so that both outwardly in our bodies, and inwardly in our souls, we may get closer and closer to Thee! (*Indignantly to the* READERS) Why the Hell don't you all say Amen?

BISHOP (*appealingly to the* YOUNG WHORE). Jannice!

YOUNG WHORE (*angrily—up to the* BISHOP). Oh, are you after me still? Go away, go away, and leave me in peace. Let me run my race in my own way. Don't be mousing after me.

BISHOP (*coming down a few steps*). I want to help you! Let me save you, Jannice.

YOUNG WHORE (*violently*). I tell you to go away. I want no God's grenadier fooling around me. (*In a half scream*) Go away!

(*The* BISHOP, *frightened, goes back above, lingering half hidden behind the War Memorial.*)

(*Recklessly as she moves about among the* READERS) I've had a few drinks, but what about it? A short life and a merry one! My heart's due to stop beating any time now, but what about it? (*She contemplates the* READERS) Devoted, body and soul, to the love of learning. Jannice's going to die dancing. (*Vehemently*) Are all you damn perishers deaf and dumb?

READERS (*in a chanting chorus*). We want to read, want to read, want to read in peace.

YOUNG WHORE (*singing recklessly*):

Stirr'd by a soft breeze in the Spring,
The blooms of an apple tree billow;
And her breast is as fragrant to me,
Looking down from the height of a pillow,
Looking down from the height of a pillow!

(*She coughs, becomes a little breathless, and presses a hand to her side.*)

I'm a sick woman. (*She bends her head down on her breast*) Death has touched me, and is telling me to be ready; take your things off, and come with me. (*Defiantly*) I'll not give in, I'll not hold back. And when I go, should God's angels beckon me up or push me down, I'll go game. (*Horrified*) Jesu, Son of Mary, what'm I saying? I'll fold all the things done in this life round me like a mantle, and wait for judgment.

(*She sinks down on a seat, and stares thoughtfully in front of her. The* POLICEWOMAN *enters, crosses over, and sees that the skirts of the* YOUNG WHORE *are a little higher than they ought to be. She stops and points her finger at the skirt. The* YOUNG WHORE *silently pulls it down. The* POLICEWOMAN *goes on.*)

VOICE READING FROM BEHIND THE WORD "MURDER". The condemned man, who is to die for cutting a woman into little bits, ate a hearty breakfast, spent an edifying hour with his chaplain, smoked a cigarette while he was being pinioned, and walked with a goose-step to the gallows.

THE REST IN CHORUS. Walked with a goose-step to the gallows.

VOICE FROM BEHIND THE WORD "SUICIDE". The dead man left a letter saying, I have owned millions; I have ruined thousands, and made many mad; I have had the honour of shaking hands with dukes and duchesses; before I put the pistol point in my ear and scatter my brains, I kiss the pictures of my little darlings, knowing that, while all men condemn, they will understand, and when they speak of me will say, he followed in the footsteps of Cato.

THE REST IN CHORUS. He followed in the footsteps of Cato.

VOICE READING FROM BEHIND THE WORD "RACING". Black cap and scarlet sleeves led for the first ten furlongs, but scarlet cap and black sleeves, coming at a hot gallop, challenged, and with a magnificent effort won by half a head.

VOICE READING FROM BEHIND THE WORD "DIVORCE". The housemaid said that she climbed the ivy, got on to the verandah, looked in through the window, saw the co-respondent in bed, the respondent in her camisole trotting towards the bed. Then came darkness, and she would leave the judge, the jury, and the counsellors to guess the rest.

THE REST IN CHORUS. Leave the judge, the jury, and the counsellors to guess the rest.

YOUNG WHORE (*rising with a half-hysterical laugh*). Never say die till you're dead. (*She contemplates the* READERS) Rape, sport, murder, and suicide. A bit of a change from the Lives of the Saints and The Acts of the Apostles! What are you all seeking? You look like a silent gang of monkeys searching for fleas.

READERS (*sticking their heads over the tops of their papers*). We want to read our papers in peace, in perfect peace.

YOUNG WHORE (*moving among them, and staggering a little as she does so*). Most important thing, too, peace, most important. That's what's wanted—peace; especially to seekers and searchers with their feet on the ground, but their heads staring at stars, composing a new hymn to intellectual beauty. Is there no one far enough from the way of the world to take an interval of rest and have a look at me?

(*She hums the Blue Danube Waltz, and dances to the tune in and out among the* READERS.)

Now you deaf and dumb perishers, have a look

at a lovely pair of legs, if you're not blind as well!

(*She lifts her skirt as she dances, quickens the time of the tune, and makes her movements keep time with the tune. The* READERS *look over the tops of their papers and watch her.*)

YOUNG WHORE. All interested now? Well, what do you think of them—saucy, eh? (*Slapping her left leg*) This one's lovely. (*Slapping the right one*) This divine!

(*She stops breathless, and scans them scornfully.*)

YOUNG WHORE (*breathless and scornful*). You bunch of high-minded toads, don't look at me long, for there's only venom for a woman in the things ye think of her. The dear joy of a sin ye turn to a sting and a bruising. (*She half sinks on a seat.*) Oh, my heart, my heart's restless again! (*She speaks in a lower tone to the* READERS.) In your looking after a woman there is no kindliness; before ye no image of loveliness, neither can ye hear the sound of a song as ye follow her, for your desire's but a venomous heat and a shame and a bruising!

(*She sinks down, pale, breathless, and frightened on the seat.*)

VOICE (*from behind the words* "*Great Cricketer*

talks about God"). The great cricketer bent to buckle his pads, saying, you may take it from me that somewhere there is a supreme, infinitely wise mind, which we call God, behind everything. God won't let the English people down —you may take that from me! He'll keep our wicket up, and the bat of faith'll drive the ball of unbelief and communism far and away beyond the fair boundary of Britain!

THE REST IN CHORUS. Far and away beyond the fair boundary of Britain!

YOUNG WHORE (*who has been moving restlessly on the seat—with frightened defiance*). I can't breathe, I can't breathe. (*She pulls open the neck of her bodice.*) It's on me again, but I'll go game, I'll go game. Eyes front, up or down.

(*The* BISHOP *comes from behind the Memorial, and slowly and timidly comes down towards the* YOUNG WHORE.)

(*In a panic of fear*) Dance, sing, and strip for the fun of the thing—that's all they want from a woman. A sigh, a sob of pain, a thought higher than their own from a woman, and they're all hurrying home. (*Turning towards the* READERS.) God damn you, will none of you stir to help when you see a Christian in danger? (*She calls*) Dreamer, Dreamer, where's the Dreamer! (*She reclines half fainting on the seat, and her words become a murmur.*) Deus, in adjutorium meum intende. Domine, ad adjuvandum me festina.

(*The* READERS *fold up their papers as she is speaking her last few sentences, and go out as they came in to staccato notes plucked from a fiddle string. When they have gone, and as the* YOUNG WHORE *is reclining on a seat in the centre, the* TWO ATTENDANTS *limp in, and throw themselves on the benches they sat on before, and sink into a drowsy slumber.*)

OLDER ATTENDANT (*sleepily*). Community singing everywhere. They won't let a man nestle dahn in peace nowhere.

(*The* BISHOP, *after hesitating several times, goes over and stands beside the* YOUNG WHORE.)

BISHOP (*softly, and with deep feeling*). You are ill, my child, and you are lonely. You have forgotten God for a moment, but He sends you His everlasting help in time of trouble, and through me, unworthy messenger, a share of His sympathy and love.

(*He sits down beside her. She recovers a little, sits up, stretches out a hand to him, which he takes and strokes gently.*)

YOUNG WHORE (*with a sigh of relief*). The heart's beating a bit steadier now, thank God.

BISHOP (*patting her hand*). That's good, now, that's good.

YOUNG WHORE (*regaining confidence, and withdrawing her hand from his*). A lot steadier now. It's more fright than anything. I get into a panic when the heart gives a double-time beat. I feel nearly normal again.

BISHOP (*encouragingly, in his pulpit manner*). That's good, my child, and shows how kind and gentle God can be to—er—a straying lamb seeking in devious ways to find a way home again to the waiting flock.

YOUNG WHORE (*fretfully*). Oh, the flock doesn't care a damn whether I'm in or out, man. The flock! So long as they get their four meals a day, with a gay hour after, and a cosy fire in the Winter, they'll never stretch a neck to see where a ram or a ewe has wandered.

BISHOP (*soothingly*). Well, never mind, now, and don't let your thoughts irritate you into any excitement, child. What you need most, now, is rest, and a chance to live a sober and a quiet life.

YOUNG WHORE (*more irritably than ever*). And follow the commandments of God—always trying to crimp people into piety. You cross, crown, and anchor boys would expect the very nightingales to warble Onward Christian Soldiers during their off-time.

BISHOP (*shocked, but trying to take it good-humouredly*). Shush, now, no excitement, please.

YOUNG WHORE (*vehemently*). I have to get a little farther away from the devil before I try to get a little nearer to God. I've a long way to travel yet before the white and holy candles are lit, and the golden incense scattered.

BISHOP. My child, the sinner is always nearer to God than the sinner dares to think.

YOUNG WHORE (*a little hysterically*). Amen, and let us get to business. Make me safe and make me happy, and I'll give sweet thanks to God. Why've you been following me about for days? I sought you once, and you sent me empty away. Why do you want to help me now?

BISHOP (*with hesitation*). Well, eh, you see, you seem to be an—eh—an interesting case. You don't seem to be an ordinary—eh—what shall I say?

YOUNG WHORE (*bitterly*). Oh, a whore. You may as well say it as think it!

(*The* BISHOP *stiffens with resentment at the girl's bluntness, and gloomily sits silent.*)

(*Looking intently at the* BISHOP) What was it

made you light on me, I wonder? There are hundreds of other girls, some of them better, a lot of them worse than me, and it's curious that I should be the lucky dip.

(*The* BISHOP *remains gloomy and silent.*)

(*After a pause*) Well, go on; open up the overture, and play us something grand.

BISHOP (*with some impatience*). My child, your present way of life's an evil way; I wish to give you a chance to turn aside from it, so please try to be decently attentive, and listen seriously to what I am about to say.

YOUNG WHORE (*with a half-suppressed giggle*). Wine's beginning to take effect again. Had a wild, wild time all this week with the Dreamer. He got an advance on a book he's getting published, and he's after another now. (*She prods the* BISHOP'S *breast.*) If he comes back before our treaty's signed, I'm off, and you won't see me till what he gets is gone. So go ahead and strike a light, and let us see the way we're walking.

BISHOP (*with gloomy indignation*). I can't listen any longer to these horrible remarks. You have no pity for yourself. You are too far away from a helping hand. (*He rises to his feet.*) I will leave you alone. I have done my best. I will leave you alone.

YOUNG WHORE (*catching his cassock—eagerly*). No, no, don't go away. I will listen, I will listen quietly, I promise. Be kind, and help me. I do want to try to do what is lawful and right. In God's name be kind, dear Bishop!

(*She pulls gently at his cassock and he slowly resumes his seat.*)

BISHOP (*rather sternly*). Listen then, child, and be serious; one more flippant word, and I leave you, never to turn a thought to you again.

YOUNG WHORE (*earnestly*). I will be serious, I promise. I fix my face, and am serious. I'll do anything you ask me to do.

BISHOP (*hesitatingly—tapping the ground with his staff*). I'm about to say something now, which, I fear, will sound very unpleasant to you, perhaps even harsh and ungenerous; something that will bite deeply into all that you may think to be a pleasure. (*He puts a hand gently and appealingly on her shoulder.*) God alone knows, my dear daughter, how deep is my desire to save you!

YOUNG WHORE. Oh, with your power and position you should be able to push me into a job that wouldn't make the change such a sad one.

BISHOP (*taking his hand from her shoulder, and speaking harshly*). I wouldn't think of getting you a place till, after a year or two's trial, I felt certain you had learned how to behave yourself.

(*A pause and a tense silence.*)

YOUNG WHORE (*with a stifled sob of humiliation*). I see.

(*Another pause.*)

How'm I to live through the two years?

BISHOP (*forcing himself to speak harshly*). I've arranged that a pious Sisterhood should receive you into their Hostel, where the Reverend Mother will care for you, watch over you, and help you to live with becoming circumspection. In return, when you begin to feel at home, you can make yourself useful to the good Sisters.

YOUNG WHORE (*with tightened lips*). I see.

(*The* POLICEWOMAN *enters, crosses in front of the* YOUNG WHORE *and the* BISHOP, *and looks fixedly and wonderingly at the pair of them. The* YOUNG WHORE *looks down at her feet and the* BISHOP *becomes interested in the top of his staff.*)

POLICEWOMAN (*speaking towards the* BISHOP). Nice die, m' lud.

BISHOP. I beg your pardon?

POLICEWOMAN. Said it was a nice die, m' lud.

BISHOP (*stammeringly*). Oh yes, quite; lovely day, beautiful day; yes, indeed, a very beautiful day.

(*The* POLICEWOMAN, *watching them as long as possible, goes slowly out.*)

BISHOP (*appealingly*). Why do you keep silent? Take your chance, take your last chance; for God's sake take your last chance.

(*The* YOUNG WHORE *sits silent.*)

Do you hear me? The offer I have made is a good offer. In it is peace, and a fair hope of better things to come. Go on, girl, speak; make up your mind, make up your mind.

YOUNG WHORE (*with hysterical laughter*). Wine's beginning to take effect again. The old mind must be worn out thinking of such a wonderful plan. He lifted me up and set me down in the midst of a holy sisterhood. Refugium peccatorum, but not for me, thank you kindly. (*She bows mockingly to the* BISHOP.) Chained fast to prayer and firm to fasting! (*She puts her face near the* BISHOP's.) Not for me, thank you kindly!

BISHOP (*with intense feeling*). What will you do when your good looks go, and you lose the means to earn your bread?

YOUNG WHORE (*with a snarling look on her face as she thrusts it close to the* BISHOP's). Die, I dare say, while you heap up hopes in the books of a bank, and carry your faith about in a coffin!

(*Up on the slope above have appeared the* TWO PLACARDED EVANGELISTS, *who stand there looking down and listening. The* TWO CHAIR ATTENDANTS *have been wakened by the loud voice of the* YOUNG WHORE *and sit listening gloatingly to the dispute between the girl and the* BISHOP. *The* YOUNG WHORE *hurriedly opens her handbag, takes out some notes and holds them close to the* BISHOP'S *nose.*)

YOUNG WHORE (*viciously*). See, old purple buttons, the last three between all I need and me! (*She rolls two of the notes into balls, and calls to the* CHAIR ATTENDANTS.) Eh, you there, up and see what God'll send you.

(*She flings a rolled-up note to each* ATTENDANT. *They open them, smooth them out, and put them joyously into their pockets.*)

(*To the Bishop*) I cling to one and fling the two others away. (*She points a finger at the* BISHOP'S *nose.*) Faith in God, old purple buttons, faith in God! Be merry, man, for a minute, for you'll be a long time dead, and it must be years and years since God heard you singing a song!

(*The* BISHOP, *with a look of sorrow, bends*

forward on the seat, and rests his head in his hands. The YOUNG WHORE *whips up his staff, and dances round with mock stateliness as she sings words to the tune of "Little Brown Jug". The* TWO PLACARDED EVANGELISTS *come half-way down and look on. The* TWO CHAIR ATTENDANTS, *as far as their game legs will allow, imitate her in a reckless manner, beating out time, one with his good right leg, and the other with his good left one.)*

YOUNG WHORE (*singing and dancing round with mock stateliness*):

Sing and dance, dance and sing,
Brief life should be a joyous thing;
The minds that are to troubles wed
Are fit to host but with the dead!
Ha ha ha, you and me, till we both have ceased
to be,
Sling out woe, hug joy instead,
For we will be a long time dead!

CHAIR ATTENDANTS (*joining vigorously in*):

Sling aht woe, 'ug joy instead,
For we will be a long time dead!

YOUNG WHORE (*singing*):

Life is born and has its day,
Sings a song, then slinks away;

Speaks a word—the word is said,—
Then hurries off to join the dead!
Ha ha ha, you and me, till we both have ceased to be,
Sling out woe, hug joy instead,
For we will be a long time dead!

CHAIR ATTENDANTS (*joining in*):
Sling aht woe, 'ug joy instead,
For we will be a long time dead.

(*As the* YOUNG WHORE *is ending the second verse of the song, the drum-tap and chant of the* DOWN-AND-OUTS *is heard faintly in the distance, coming nearer and nearer. The* EVANGELISTS *hear it first, and lean their heads in the direction of the sound, with fright on their faces. Then the* CHAIR ATTENDANTS *hear it, stiffen, and end the chorus weakly. The* YOUNG WHORE *hears it last, and stands stiff, frightened and listening intently.*)

ALL (*speaking together, except the* BISHOP). The drum-beat and chant of the Down-and-Outs!

(*The birds, which have begun to sing at the beginning of the song sung by the* YOUNG WHORE, *become silent; the scene seems to grow dark and chilly, and the*

BISHOP *shivers. The sky changes to a bright grey, and against this grey sky the black silhouettes of the* DOWN-AND-OUTS *pass by. They are bent, tattered, and hopeless wrecks of old and young men and women; they go by in a slow and miserable manner, chanting their miserere to the monotonous tap, tap, tap of the drum-beat.*)

DOWN-AND-OUTS (*chanting*):

We challenge life no more, no more, with our dead faith, or a dead hope;
We carry furl'd the fainting flag of a dead hope and a dead faith.
Day sings no song, neither is there room for rest beside night in her sleeping;
We've but a sigh for a song, and a deep sigh for a drum-beat.
Oh where shall we go when the day calls?
Oh where shall we sleep when the night falls?
We've but a sigh for a song, and a deep sigh for a drum-beat!

(*The silhouettes of the* DOWN-AND-OUTS *pass out, their song fading out in the repetition of the line, "we've but a sigh for a song, and a deep sigh for a drum-beat".*)

BISHOP (*lifting the staff, which he has taken*

from the YOUNG WHORE, *above his head*). There go the poor, the sacred aristocracy of God! Join them, my children, in self-abasement, and find a sharp penitence and a sweet peace!

(*The scene becomes as bright and sunny as before, and the birds begin to sing again.*)

PLACARDED EVANGELISTS (*together, angrily down to the* BISHOP). Wot'r you torking abaht? Call o' the Dahn-en'-Ahts don't apply to us; both of us is in the 'ands of Gord already!

(*They go off, one to the right, the other to the left, bent-backed and frightened.*)

CHAIR ATTENDANTS (*together, angrily to the* BISHOP). 'Ere, you mind your own business, see, ecclesiastical Mickey Mouse! Th' offer t' join your maundy menagerie's declined, see? (*As they go out, one to the left, the other to the right*) Dahn-en'-Ahts ain't alooking for us!

(*The* YOUNG WHORE *goes to a seat and sits down dejectedly; the* BISHOP *comes close to her.*)

BISHOP. And you? They came close, my child, they came close. They will get you some day, if you do not let me save you now. The day is fair, my daughter, the day is fair, but what of the night, when youth has faded, and the shadows fall, and the heart is lonely?

YOUNG WHORE (*tonelessly, but defiantly*). When

youth has gone; when night has fallen, and when the heart is lonely, I will stand and stare steady at a god who has filled the wealthy with good things, and has sent the poor empty away.

BISHOP (*sorrowfully*). Don't say such things, child. Come with me, I beg of you to come with me.

YOUNG WHORE (*with tight lips*). No.

(*The* BISHOP *looks sadly at her for a moment, then turns and goes slowly up the slope. When more than half-way up, he turns, and speaks pleadingly down to the* YOUNG WHORE.)

BISHOP (*making the sign of the cross*). My poor child, I ask you in the name of God; come!

YOUNG WHORE (*firmly, though her lips quiver a little*). No!

(*The* BISHOP *looks at her for a moment, then turns and goes slowly out. The* YOUNG WHORE *reclines back on the seat, and sits silent and desolate looking. The birds sing for a few moments. From the right a man—it is the* FOREMAN—*enters. He is off duty, and has cast off his dungarees, and is nattily dressed, with a sober black suit, black bowler hat, high white collar, and carries a pair of gloves. He is fol-*

lowed by a short, stocky man, whose legs when they are together are as thick as his trunk. He has a white moustache, and his face wears an impatient look, as if he anticipated every argument a disputant would say. He carries a short, stout stick, and has a habit, as he listens to what is being said, of turning impatiently and slowly round, tapping the ground with his stick as he does so. The ATHEIST *immediately follows him. People have begun to stroll about the scene from various points, and in every direction.)*

MAN WITH THE STICK (*calling scornfully after the* FOREMAN). Eh, man, stan' your ground, stan' your ground; don't go en' gallop off when you're cornered!

(*The* FOREMAN *hesitates at the challenge, and the* ATHEIST *and the* MAN WITH THE STICK *catch up with him, and with other listeners form a group in the centre.)*

FOREMAN. If we're agoing to carry on the discussion, let's 'ave no mockery.

MAN WITH THE STICK (*apologetically*). Righto, I'm silent. (*Indicating the* ATHEIST) I'll leave it to 'im—'e'll do the trick proper.

ATHEIST (*gently to the* FOREMAN). Go on, brother, let's 'ear your postulation.

FOREMAN. Well, I says use your eyes, use your ears, use your brine, en' wot's the explanytion of the wunnderful things arahnd us—on the earth, en' above us in the sky—en' I say Gord myde them orl.

MAN WITH THE STICK (*with a short, scornful laugh*). En' 'oo myde Gord?

ATHEIST (*to the* MAN WITH THE STICK). Give 'im a charnce, brother.

FOREMAN (*to the* MAN WITH THE STICK). 'E alwyes existed. In the beginning all things was myde by 'im, en' withaht 'im was not enything myde wot was myde.

MAN WITH THE STICK (*tapping the ground with his stick and turning till his back is almost turned to the disputants—with unutterable scorn*). Aw, Genesis!

ATHEIST (*quietly and firmly*). There never was a beginning, brother. Nothing 'as been myde, en' everything's evolved aht of matter, energy, en' force; forms chynging, but substance remyning the syme.

MAN WITH THE STICK (*tapping the ground, and turning round*). 'Course they 'as.

FOREMAN (*hesitatingly*). Yes, in a wye, yes; but even Einstein says——

MAN WITH THE STICK (*interrupting explosively*). Aw, we're not responsible for wot Einstein says!

ATHEIST (*deprecatingly to the* MAN WITH THE STICK). Shush, brother.

FOREMAN (*stammeringly*). Wot first creayted this matter en' this energy en' this force we speak abaht? If it was alwyes, 'ow was it alwyes, en' where was it alwyes? We gets nowhere when we says thet wot's to come comes aht of wot is, en' wot is, is aht of wot was; so I says behind everything is, en' was, a Gord!

MAN WITH THE STICK (*explosively*). Aw, Genesis agine! (*Turning and tapping the ground with his stick*) Try to get Gord aht of your mind, man. (*To the* ATHEIST) 'E'll never get nowhere in thought till 'e gets rid of the idear of Gord aht of 'is mind—Gord an' Genesis!

ATHEIST (*angrily to the* MAN WITH THE STICK). Oh, give 'im en' me a charnce, will you?

MAN WITH THE STICK. Yes, but we warnt proof, en' not hearsay. (*To the* FOREMAN) Proof, give us proof, man; that's wot we warnt —proof.

FOREMAN. Wot I says is thet everyone's againe veering rahnd to the idear of a power ahtside of wot we see, en' 'ear, en' 'andle. In recent writings even a prominent politician's beginning to realise the necessity for the belief in Gord.

MAN WITH THE STICK (*vehemently*). Politician—nime, nime, nime!

FOREMAN. I read th' other dye thet a clergyman said thet it was the opinion of the Right Honourable Winston Churchill——

MAN WITH THE STICK (*interrupting violently*). Winstn Churchill! Why do you bring irrelevant trivialities into the discussion, man? (*He turns till his back is turned to the* FOREMAN, *tapping the ground indignantly with his stick.*) Aw, Genesis on the one hand and Winstn Churchill on the other, wha'! (*He turns back again.*) Y'll never get intensity of thought, man, if you don't learn to think for yourself!

(*A group of people, men and women, has collected behind the speakers, among which are several in the uniform of the Salvation Army. Behind this group is raised the red and blue banner of the sect. The* YOUNG SALVATION ARMY OFFICER *has entered, and halted to listen for a few moments to the disputants.*)

ATHEIST (*to the* FOREMAN). Brother, there never was a time when nothing was.

Y.S.A. OFFICER (*butting in quickly*). You're

right, brother; God is from everlasting to everlasting, Alleluiah!

MAN WITH THE STICK (*explosively—glancing at the* SALVATION ARMY OFFICER). Aw, 'ere's the storm troops dahn on top of us now!

(*The* YOUNG WHORE *suddenly bursts through the group of speakers. She is excited, and she scatters them in a reckless manner.*)

YOUNG WHORE (*excitedly speaking to everyone in general*). Give us a song, for God's sake! Heart ready to stop beating any second, but game for anything. If I die, I'll go game, and die dancing.

(*The* ATHEIST, *the* FOREMAN, *and the* MAN WITH THE STICK *have slipped out of her reach, and stand in the* CROWD, *watching all that happens. The* YOUNG WHORE *puts her arms around the* SALVATION ARMY OFFICER.)

YOUNG WHORE (*recklessly to the* OFFICER). Get out of the gloom for a minute, dear; come into the sun, and kiss me with the kisses of thy mouth!

Y.S.A. OFFICER (*gently to the* YOUNG WHORE). We desire not the knowledge of thy ways, sister, but rather seek to grow in knowledge of our Lord Jesus Christ.

YOUNG WHORE (*recklessly*). Dance and drink; sing and be sad, for to-morrow we die!

Y.S.A. OFFICER (*gently removing the* YOUNG WHORE'S *arms from about him*). God grant thee mercy, sister, before He brings thee unto judgment.

(*The* YOUNG SALVATION ARMY OFFICER *goes over to the* CROWD *and mounts a portable platform in the centre of the semicircle that the* CROWD *forms. Behind him is the banner; to his right, one of the* PLACARDED EVANGELISTS; *to his left, the other. At the right point of the semicircle is the* OLDER CHAIR ATTENDANT, *at the left point, the* YOUNGER CHAIR ATTENDANT. *Behind the* CROWD, *watching, are the* ATHEIST, *the* FOREMAN, *the* MAN WITH THE STICK, *and a little to the front the* YOUNG MAN IN PLUS-FOURS. *The* SALVATION ARMY OFFICER *bows his head for a moment in silent prayer, then looks over the* CROWD, *casting a longing glance in the direction of the* YOUNG WHORE. *He stands erect, slowly stretches his arms wide in the symbol of a cross, and speaks to those around him.*)

Y.S.A. OFFICER. The one hope of the poor

sinner is the cross. We must struggle down to the cross before we can climb up to the crown. There are sinners with us to-night who need the pardon Christ can give: Let them come to the foot of the Cross. There are sinners here who, in the hot laughter of sin, need the peace of God in their hearts: Let them come to the foot of the Cross. Brothers and sisters, let us pray that they may turn aside from their sin and be saved! (*He looks upwards and lifts his arms appealingly.*) Lord God Almighty, stretch out Thine arms and save those who are lost in trespasses and sins!

SALVATIONISTS (*in chorus*). Save them, great and most merciful Redeemer.

Y.S.A. OFFICER. That the trumpets of the angels may have a new and joyful note in their sounding!

SALVATIONISTS (*in chorus*). Save them, great and most merciful Redeemer.

Y.S.A. OFFICER. That the crown of thorns on the head of the crucified one may shine as the sun on a noon in the season of Summer!

SALVATIONISTS (*in chorus*). Save them, great and most merciful Redeemer.

Y.S.A. OFFICER. That the nails in His hands and His feet may gleam like the moon at the full in the season of harvest!

SALVATIONISTS (*in chorus*). Save them, great and most merciful Redeemer.

(*The* YOUNG WHORE *has listened from the first; then she has become interested; then deeply moved. She has come closer and closer to the front till she stands almost in front of the speaker. She has joined with the* SALVATIONISTS *in the last petition, and now, in a sudden movement, goes to the mat stretched in front of the portable platform, and kneels down on it, shaken with emotion.*)

YOUNG WHORE (*brokenly*). Great and most merciful Redeemer, save me!

SALVATIONISTS (*in chorus*). Save her, great and most merciful Redeemer.

YOUNG WHORE (*wildly*). He will not hear me. He will not hear me! I'm a whore too deeply trenched in sin to be saved!

SALVATIONISTS (*in chorus*). Save her, save her, great and most merciful Redeemer.

MAN WITH THE STICK (*mockingly—from among the crowd*). I thought she said she'd die darncing!

(*The* CHAIR ATTENDANTS *slink over and kneel on the mat, one on each side of the* YOUNG WHORE, *with hands clasped and heads bent. A look of pride comes over the face of the* YOUNG OFFICER.)

YOUNG WHORE (*moaningly*). I see the wrath of God flaming in front of me. Save me, oh, save me, from the fire that can never be quenched!

(*The* YOUNG OFFICER *steps from the platform, comes close to the sinners, and places a hand gently on the* YOUNG WHORE'S *head.*)

Y.S.A. OFFICER (*to the* YOUNG WHORE). Be of good comfort, sister; only believe, and thou shalt be saved. The Kingdom of heaven with all its pardon, and all its peace, its power, and all its glory, is in the first thought a sinner gives to God!

(*While the* OFFICER *is speaking, the* SCARLET WOMAN, *with a stylised smile on her face, enters, pauses a moment to look at the meeting, sees the* YOUNG MAN IN PLUS-FOURS, *gives him a glance, and then goes up the centre to the slope, passes over and goes out. The* YOUNG MAN IN PLUS-FOURS, *who has returned her glance, moves gradually back till he is free from the* CROWD, *saunters slowly to the centre, then quickening his pace, hurries out after the* SCARLET WOMAN.

The OFFICER, *who has his left hand on the head of the* YOUNG WHORE, *raises his right one, and gently beating out the first few notes of the tune, begins to sing softly.*)

Y.S.A. OFFICER (*singing*):

Before Thy Cross, O Lord, we bow,
And claim Thy faithful promise now:
These sin-red souls make white as snow,
That they Thy peace may know.

SALVATIONISTS (*in chorus*):

These sin-red souls make white as snow,
That they Thy peace may know.

Y.S.A. OFFICER (*singing*):

Show, Lord, the calm of Calvary,
To frightened souls that cry to Thee;
Cag'd fast in doubt, half-mad with fear—
Oh, bring Thy pardon near.

SALVATIONISTS (*in chorus*):

Cag'd fast in doubt, half-mad with fear—
Oh, bring Thy pardon near!

(*Above on the slope, looking around him, appears the* DREAMER. *He is flushed with suppressed excitement.*)

YOUNG WHORE (*piteously*). Oh, great and most merciful Redeemer, hide me from the glow of the fire that can never be quenched!

(*The* DREAMER *hears the voice of the*

YOUNG WHORE, *looks down to where the meeting is being held, and calls her name. She starts when she hears his voice, makes a movement to rise, but the hand of the* YOUNG OFFICER *is on her head, and she remains on her knees.*)

DREAMER (*calling loudly*). Jannice! Jannice!

(*The* YOUNG WHORE *gives a start when she hears her name called, and rises to her feet, hesitates, then stands with her head bent on her breast.*)

(*Joyously down to the* YOUNG WHORE) I have that will give another month of gay and crowded life of wine and laughter; joy in our going out and our coming in, and the dear pain from the golden flame of love. Jannice, Jannice, the Dreamer calls!

(*The* YOUNG WHORE *turns to go, but the* YOUNG SALVATION ARMY OFFICER *lays a restraining hand upon her shoulder.*)

Y.S.A. OFFICER (*singing*):

Long blind in sin, now let them see
The loveliness of life in Thee;
For fleshly joys and worldly gain
End soon in unending pain.

SALVATIONISTS (*in chorus*):

For fleshly joys and worldly gain
End soon in unending pain!

(*The* CHAIR ATTENDANTS *squirm round on their knees, and spread out the fingers of their hands which cover their faces, so as to watch the actions of the* YOUNG WHORE, *who backs a little away from the meeting's circle towards the centre. The* YOUNG OFFICER *puts his hands over his face in a reverential attitude of prayer. The* DREAMER *comes a little way down the slope with his eyes fixed on the* YOUNG WHORE.)

Y.S.A. OFFICER (*covering his face with his hands and bending his head*). Let us pray silently and together for the soul of this young girl.

(*All the* SALVATIONISTS *and most of the* CROWD *cover their faces with their hands and bend their heads.*)

DREAMER (*calling to the* YOUNG WHORE). The Dreamer calls you to the deep kiss and the clutch of love; to sing our song with the song that is sung by a thousand stars of the evening!

(*The* YOUNG WHORE *retires slowly away from the praying group while the* DREAMER *is speaking, gradually quickening her movement till, reaching the centre path, she runs up into his arms, and the two cross over the slope and go out together.*

The two kneeling CHAIR ATTENDANTS *stretch their necks to follow the* YOUNG WHORE'S *movements. After a slight pause, the* YOUNG OFFICER *takes his hands from his face, and lifts his head, followed by all who have acted similarly. The* TWO CHAIR ATTENDANTS *at once resume their prayerful attitude. The* YOUNG OFFICER *sees that the girl has gone, and, with an effort, resumes control of the meeting.*)

Y.S.A. OFFICER (*singing a little dejectedly and in low tones*):
Oh, let Thy mercy follow swift
The sinner who rejects Thy gift.
Show her who rudely runs astray
The truth, the life, the way.

SALVATIONISTS (*in chorus—very softly*):
Show her who rudely runs astray
The truth, the life, the way!

MAN WITH THE STICK (*mockingly*). She must ha' gorn to die darncing!

THE GATES CLOSE

SCENE IV

Winter.

It is night-time.

The colour of the sky is a deep black, brightening from the centre to the horizon into a rich purple hue.

To the right, where the purple sky begins to fade into blackness, is a group of stars, one red, one golden, and the rest silver. The trees are bare of leaves, and their branches form a silvery pattern against the purple and black of the sky.

Light from an electric lamp behind the War Memorial shines on the head and shoulders of the figure, making them glow like aluminium, and the bent head appears to be looking down on the life going on below from the depths of the black sky. The cries of the gulls heard occasionally over the lake are shrill and penetrating. To the right is a portable platform with a rail or ledge on which to lean or place a book or papers. Another of these platforms stands on the left.

A SPEAKER *on each is clapping his hands against his shoulders to take away the numbness.*

After a few moments of this exercise, they lean idly over the platform ledge watching vacantly the few people who are walking about, waiting for someone to pause in front of them before beginning to speak.

Hanging on the platform of the 2ND PLATFORM SPEAKER *is a notice on which are the words: " There Must be a God "; on the other platform, a notice with the words: "There can't be a God".*

Occasionally they get down from their platforms, walk about, and clap their hands on their shoulders to keep the blood circulating.

The BISHOP *is seen above, coming from behind the Memorial. He stands there, and looks anxiously around, then comes down quickly, hurries to the left, pauses, then turns and goes out hurriedly by the right.*

The TWO MEN *on the platforms watch his movements, and look after him when he goes out.*

1ST PLATFORM SPEAKER (*to the* SPEAKER *on his right*). Wunner wot 'e's after? Been dodging backwards and forwards for hours.

2ND PLATFORM SPEAKER. Dunno. (*Emphatically*) En' I don't cire!

1ST PLATFORM SPEAKER. Notice that 'e's a Bishop? I've seen 'im in questionable company, too, brother. You should speak seriously to him, brother, for a bishop must be blameless.

2ND PLATFORM SPEAKER (*surlily*). I'm not 'ere to prove the blimelessness of bishops.

1ST PLATFORM SPEAKER (*mockingly*). No? Tike up too much time, I suppose. (*A pause.*) Must be a wearing thing to be trying to prove Christianity in a Christian country.

(*The* MAN WITH THE STICK *enters, pauses, and looks at the notice hanging on the platform of the* 2ND SPEAKER.)

MAN WITH THE STICK (*reading the notice*). Huh!

2ND PLATFORM SPEAKER (*rousing himself and beginning to address the* MAN WITH THE STICK). The Christian Evidence Guild keeps its flag flying in Summer en' Winter.

MAN WITH THE STICK (*butting in*). Excuse me, Mr. Speaker; do you believe thet the Ten Commandments constitoot a competent rule of life en' conduct?

2ND PLATFORM SPEAKER (*hesitatingly*). Well, er, generally speaking, yes.

MAN WITH THE STICK. Sure?

2ND PLATFORM SPEAKER. I'd sye so.

MAN WITH THE STICK. Christian countries

don't seem to think so, then, for even England, during the last thirty years, 'as mide over two thousand lawrs, covering sixteen thousand pyges of cep imperial octavo, which is quite a tidy addition to the lawr of loving your nighbour as yourself.

2ND PLATFORM SPEAKER. Oh, I didn't know thet, friend.

MAN WITH THE STICK. Well, you know it now.

(*He goes up and across the slope and out.*)

1ST PLATFORM SPEAKER (*mockingly*). Get thet, brother? En' they 'aven't finished miking new lawrs yet to 'elp the Ten Commandments aht. By the time they mike another two thousand, we'll all be well in the wood.

(*The* BISHOP'S SISTER *enters hurriedly on the slope above, and looks anxiously round her.*)

BISHOP'S SISTER (*calling loudly*). Gilbert, Gilbert, where are you? Gilbert!

(*She comes quickly down to the front between the two platforms—looks to the right, then to the left, and runs back again, crosses the slope and goes out.*)

1ST PLATFORM SPEAKER (*reflectively*). Who's she after now? Gilbert—wunner who's Gilbert?

2ND PLATFORM SPEAKER (*gloomily*). Don't know. (*Emphatically*) En' I don't cire.

1ST PLATFORM SPEAKER. There's not much melody in your mike-up for one who knows Gord is, en' cires. . . . See where the Bishops warnted to put in The Form of Prayer a petition to Gord asking 'im to grant the restorytion of credit? " By the confidence of restored credit, give us our diely bread." Fawncy asking Gord for credit!

2ND PLATFORM SPEAKER (*with intense loathing*). I scorns you! Russia's your country—thet's where you ought to be—Russia. You'd know then wot it was to live in a country withaht Gord.

1ST PLATFORM SPEAKER (*calmly*). If it's no better than a country wot 'as a Gord, then it must be a terrible plice.

2ND PLATFORM SPEAKER (*heatedly*). Withaht Gord en' withaht bread; sterving, sterving, sterving!

1ST PLATFORM SPEAKER (*quietly*). I'd just as soon sterve in Russia because food is scarce, as sterve in a country ahtside Russia because food is plentiful.

2ND PLATFORM SPEAKER (*leaning over towards* 1ST SPEAKER *and speaking heatedly*). I scorns you, scorns you utterly, en' withaht malice.

Wot I says is thet legislytion should be interdooced to mike such persons as you worship publicly whether you like it or not; en' it'll be done, sooner or lyter.

1ST PLATFORM SPEAKER (*with provoking calmness*). Downt get mad, brother.

2ND PLATFORM SPEAKER (*violently*). I'm not mad, not a bit of it. Just indignant, thet's all. You Atheists er' all brayenbrag while you're feeling sife, but you soon get eager f'r the Christian 'ope when your time comes to go!

1ST PLATFORM SPEAKER (*flaring up*). Who gets eager for the Christian 'ope when 'is time 'as come to go! Wot 'ope? Nice sort of 'ope to 'ope for when a man 'as to go! The last defamytion of the last minutes of an Atheist's life. If wot you 'old is true, then the last 'ope the Atheist'd 'ope to 'ave when 'e was abaht to go, is the Christian 'ope of 'aving to meet 'is miker.

2ND PLATFORM SPEAKER (*mockingly*). Don't get mad, brother.

1ST PLATFORM SPEAKER (*raging*). Oh, you mike me larf!

(*A group in the core of which are two disputants, enter and cross over in slow, rhythmic movements, a step or so at a time, so as to allow all they have to say being said before they pass out at the opposite side to that by which they came in. Every member of the group is covered with a top-coat, the collars pulled up as high as they will go, and they are all shivering a little.*

One of the disputants wears a bowler hat, and has an umbrella under one arm.

The other wears a trilby hat, and carries a pair of pince-nez balanced on his nose.

Behind, pressing in on the group, eager to hear all that is said, is the MAN WITH THE STICK.

MAN IN THE TRILBY, *as he comes in*—)

MAN IN THE TRILBY. Yes, quite; I get that, but——

MAN IN BOWLER HAT (*interrupting*). Wait, hold on a second. Don't question me, yet. Listen carefully; let your mind follow what I say, and you'll get the idea.

MAN WITH THE STICK (*from behind*). Listen cautiously to wot the gentleman's a-saying; 'e knows wot 'e's torking abaht.

MAN IN THE BOWLER HAT. Now try to remember that all the old ideas of the cosmos are buried with Copernicus, Kepler, Newton, en' all that crew.

MAN WITH THE STICK. Ay, en' buried deep, too.

MAN WITH THE BOWLER HAT. Now we all know that the clock created time, and the measuring-rod created spice, so that there is really neither spice nor time; but there is such a thing as spice-time. Get that?

MAN IN THE TRILBY HAT (*with confidence*). Quite; that much is perfectly clear.

MAN IN THE BOWLER HAT. Right. Now supposing that one night while we all slept, the universe sank down to the size of a football, en' all the clocks began to move a thousand times slower, it wouldn't make the slightest difference to us, for we wouldn't realise that any change had taken place, though each of us would live a thousand times longer, and man couldn't be seen, even under a microscope.

VOICE FROM THE GROUP. Could a woman be seen under a microscope?

MAN WITH THE STICK (*with angry impatience at the interruption*). Aw!

MAN IN THE BOWLER HAT (*remonstratively*). Levity's out of place, friend, when men are trying to think out the truth of things.

VOICE FROM THE GROUP. Yes, but 'ow could the universe suddenly shrink dahn to the size of a football?

MAN IN THE BOWLER HAT. I said *if* it did, friend.

VOICE FROM THE GROUP. Oh, ay, if—a big if, I'd say!

MAN WITH THE STICK (*impatiently turning, and tapping the ground with his stick*). Aw!

MAN IN THE TRILBY (*patronisingly to the* VOICE). Our friend's just raising an hypothenuse, just an hypothenuse, nothing more.

MAN IN THE BOWLER HAT (*to the* MAN IN THE TRILBY). Well, friend, do you get the synoptic idea?

MAN IN THE TRILBY (*dubiously*). It's a presumptuous postulatum, en' requires quite a lot of thinking out.

MAN WITH THE STICK (*dogmatically*). It's as simple, man, as A B C said backwards. You've got your mind crahded with the dialectics of Genesis, en' all thet sort of stuff. We're dealing now with a spice-time problem; not time en' spice, but spice-time; see?

(*They all pass out.*)

(*As the disputants go out—the* BISHOP *appears from behind the Memorial. He hurries down to the front, and is followed by his* SISTER. *He stands and looks anxiously to the left and right. His* SISTER, *looking worried and dis-*

tressed, comes up to him and catches his arm.)

BISHOP'S SISTER (*imploringly*). For God's sake, give it up, Gilbert. You've been racing round after the creature for more than an hour. You're not even sure she's in the Park. (*Venomously*) Probably away with one of her terrible men. I'll leave you if you go on like this any longer.

BISHOP (*tonelessly*). Leave me then. If she's not here, I'll wait till she comes back. (*Suddenly catching her arm and pointing out from him*) Look—that girl going down the path there; is that she? She'll be going through the light from a lamp in a second, and my eyes are too dim to be sure. (*A short pause.*) Now; quick, quick, look, can't you, and tell me if it's she!

BISHOP'S SISTER (*stormily*). I won't, I won't look. Think of what you're doing, Gilbert: help and kindness are only tortures to creatures of her kind. (*She catches his arm, and tries to drag him away.*) Please, please, come home, and be sensible.

(*He shakes her hand off his arm, and hurries out in the direction of where he thinks he saw the girl.*

The BISHOP'S SISTER *stands motionless for*

a second, then distractedly follows him out.)

BISHOP'S SISTER (*imploringly calling after the* BISHOP *as she hurries out*). Gilbert!

(*The* TWO PLATFORM SPEAKERS *who have been watching and listening, stretch over their platforms as far as safety will permit, and peer after the* BISHOP *and his* SISTER.

After a few moments, they resume their former positions, and begin to clap their hands against their shoulders to warm them.)

1ST PLATFORM SPEAKER (*meaningly*). There you are, there's a model of one chosen, with the ide of pryer en' fasting, to guide our feet into the way of peace.

(*The* YOUNG MAN IN PLUS-FOURS *enters upon the slope above, and gazes vacantly round him.*)

2ND PLATFORM SPEAKER (*venomously*). Ex nihilo nihil fit: that's your cap-badge, see? Wot yeh warnt to always plenk your pitch on top of mine for?

(*The* YOUNG MAN IN PLUS-FOURS *comes down in an aimless way, stops before the platform of the* 1ST SPEAKER, *and stares at the notice. The* 1ST PLATFORM

SPEAKER, *after a few moments' pause, leans over and begins to direct his remarks to him. Just as he begins to speak, the* SCARLET WOMAN *comes in, stops before the* 2ND PLATFORM SPEAKER *and stares at the notice. The* 2ND PLATFORM SPEAKER *begins to direct remarks at her, so that he and the* 1ST PLATFORM SPEAKER *speak together.*)

1ST PLATFORM SPEAKER and 2ND PLATFORM SPEAKER (*together*) There isn't a clime Christianity mikes thet can be substanteeyted.
Summer en' Winter the Christian Evidence Guild keeps the flag flying.

(*As they speak, the* SCARLET WOMAN, *having eyed the* YOUNG MAN IN PLUS-FOURS *goes out, and he follows her.*

The TWO SPEAKERS *resume their lazy pose on the ledges of the platform as the* OLD WOMAN *comes in slowly and wearily, sagging a little in the middle. She looks vacantly up at the* 2ND SPEAKER *on the platform and pauses before him.*

He rouses himself when he notices that somebody has halted in front of him, and maybe prepared to listen. He leans forward, looks at her fixedly and begins to speak.)

2ND PLATFORM SPEAKER. In Summer en' Winter the Christian Evidence Guild keeps its flag flying. Two things, Nyture en' man—speaking on a low pline—comprise all we know, see, en' feel. Now Nyture's orlright, perducing abundantly all that man requires. Nyture's orlright, so wot's left? Man. I know man's a part of Nyture, but a part to which Gord's given a lofty mind en' a mighty understandin'.

OLD WOMAN (*tonelessly*). Everything golden's gone into the bellies of the worms.

2ND PLATFORM SPEAKER (*failing to hear what she has said*). Beg pawdn?

OLD WOMAN. I never have to raise my voice, for God can hear a whisper as well, and better even than a thunderclap. Yet a little while and He'll level down to nothing the stir that still remains around us; for all the gold of England's life is tarnishing now in the bellies of the worms!

(*She wanders over to the* 1ST PLATFORM SPEAKER, *pauses, and looks vacantly up at him.*

The SPEAKER *rouses himself, looks down at the* OLD WOMAN *and begins to speak.*)

1ST PLATFORM SPEAKER. There isn't a clime that Christianity mikes that can be substanteeyted.

Mark contradicting Matthew, Luke doing the sime to Mark, en' John on his own, contradicting all the others. Any scholar'll tell you it all comes aht of the Egyptian Book of the Dead. If I was to dive deep into things en' tell you the original meaning of so-called Christian symbols, I'd be arrested in double-quick time. But wot I wants to point aht en' prove is that Christianity's a noosance; from Quakerism to Psychopannychism, it's a noosance, en' in the wye of power, politics, en' ply.

OLD WOMAN (*speaking tonelessly up to the* SPEAKER). There can be nor rest nor work nor play where there is no life, and the golden infancy of England's life is tarnishing now in the bellies of the worms.

2ND PLATFORM SPEAKER (*bending down towards her*). Beg pawdn, mad'm?

OLD WOMAN (*murmuringly*). Your politics are husks that only swine will eat; your power's behind a battlement of hunger; your religion's as holy as a coloured garter round a whore's thigh; truth's bent in two, and hope is broken. (*She begins to wander away.*) O Jesus, is there no wisdom to be found anywhere! All gone with the golden life of England into the bellies of the worms!

(*She goes out slowly and with tired steps.*

The TWO SPEAKERS, *after leaning lazily on the ledges of their platforms, rise and climb down, just as* TWO COUPLES, *one a civilian and the* 2ND NURSEMAID; *the other the* 1ST NURSEMAID *and the* GUARDSMAN, *appear on slope above and come down the centre path; one* COUPLE *goes to the left, the other to the right, then both stop and stand with their arms round each other.*)

1ST PLATFORM SPEAKER (*half to himself, and half to the other* SPEAKER). No use this pitch; I'm going higher up.

2ND PLATFORM SPEAKER. No use, this pitch; I'm going lower down.

(*They fold up their platforms, and, crossing by each other, go out their several ways.*)

GUARDSMAN (*to his girl*). Company Sergeant-Myjor's a fire terror 'e is. Gives you a feelin' 'e 'ites everyone, 'e does, en' wishes you was dead. Wye 'e prods you when 'e 'as a complynt to mike, gets you on the rawr, 'e does. I'm the only one in the compny as tells 'im orf.

1ST NURSEMAID (*gurglingly*). G's another squeeze, Frankie!

GUARDSMAN. Eh? (*catching her meaning*). Oh, righto.

(*He gives her a long and vigorous squeeze, with a kiss thrown in.*)

1ST NURSEMAID (*in ecstasy*). Ohoo, lovely.

GUARDSMAN (*relapsing into his previous interest*). Other dy 'e says, 'ere, Guardsman Gunn, wot's the meaning of your bed not being properly folded? Git yer mind movin', 'e roars, git yer mind movin' for Gord's sike, en' give yer reason fer not 'avin' yer bed properly folded!

1ST NURSEMAID. Ign'rant barstid!

GUARDSMAN. 'Ere, 'e ses, corpr'l, fetch a chire, so's I c'n sit dahn en' wite while Guardsman Gunn's thinkin' aht 'is stytement.

1ST NURSEMAID. 'Orrible, en' you 'avin' to stend dumb in front of 'im, wha'?

(YOUNG MAN, *on the left, with his arm round the* NURSEMAID—)

YOUNG MAN. Fire nawseeyting it was. We've no right, 'e ses, to be in Indiar. Indians, 'e ses, is repressed en' kep' back from eddicyting theirselves. Withaht us, 'e ses, they'd 'ave edvenced proper.

2ND NURSEMAID. Stoopid idear. Wunner wot they would 'ave done withaht our 'elp 'en eddicytion?

YOUNG MAN (*vauntingly*). 'Ere, Mr. Speaker, I ses, 'olding up my 'and so thet the crahd turned their 'eads in my direction.

2ND NURSEMAID (*gushingly*). Gis another squeeze, Jack.

YOUNG MAN. Wha'? (*Realising what she wants.*) Oh, righto.

(*He tightens her to him, and gives her a kiss.*)

2ND NURSEMAID (*in ecstasy*). Oh oo!

YOUNG MAN (*resuming the subject*). Mr. Speaker, I ses, d'ja know wot yer torking abaht? Wot abaht China? Call the Chinks intelligent? 'Oo interfered with them, en' yet they carn't do nothing of theirselves. I've 'eard they've done a few fine things in their dy, but everybody knows as 'ow they 'aven't edvenced a step in a thousand years.

2ND NURSEMAID. Gorn back, I'd sy.

YOUNG MAN. 'Course they 'as!

2ND NURSEMAID. Gis another squeeze, Jack.

YOUNG MAN. Wha'? Oh, righto. (*He squeezes her to him.*) Y' should ha' seen 'is fice when 'e sawr I 'ad 'im cornered.

2ND NURSEMAID. Like an angel agoing to sneeze, wha'? Tighten me up agine, darling.

(*He kisses her and tightens his arms around her.*)

1ST NURSEMAID (*to the* GUARDSMAN). G'wye, you didn't!

GUARDSMAN (*boastingly*). Didn't I though.

Gits 'old of a b'ynet en' chised 'im full gallop rahnd the barrack squire till I was caught en' 'eld by the picquet.

1ST NURSEMAID. Cells for you, Frankie.

GUARDSMAN. When I was 'auled up before Myjor, 'e did look fierce, my oath, 'e did. Serious breach of discipline, 'e ses. Considering the provocytion, admonished, I think, will meet the cise. En' agoing aht, 'e ses to me, private like, served 'im right, Guardsman, served 'im right; pity you didn't give 'im a jab, 'e ses,—I know the bugger.

1ST NURSEMAID (*dreamily*). Real, live gennelman, th' Major, wha'?

GUARDSMAN. A torf.

(*As the* TWO COUPLES *are embracing with warmth and goodwill, the* OLD WOMAN *appears, before the figure of the Memorial. She remains silent for a moment, with head bent, then begins to speak tonelessly and sadly.*

The COUPLES, *when they hear her speaking, loosen their arms a little from round each other.*)

OLD WOMAN. A few more moments of time, an' Spring'll be dancin' among us again; dancin' in golden an' purple pavilions 'f laburnum an' lilac; the birds'll be busy at buildin' small worlds of their own in the safe an' snug breast of the hedges; the girls will go ramblin' around, all big with the thought of the life in the loins of the young men; but those who are gone shall sink into stillness, deep under the stillness that shelters the dead.

YOUNG MAN (*over to the* GUARDSMAN). What abaht goin' to the bushes at the bird sanctuary, Frank?

1ST NURSEMAID. An' tell stories withaht eny words, wha'?

(*The* OLD WOMAN *lifts the wreath she is carrying, elevating it as a priest elevates the Host.*)

OLD WOMAN (*facing the Memorial Figure*). O soldier in bronze, cold guard of remembrance for those who rode out on swift horses to battle and fell, I lay at thy feet this circle of green and ribbon of red, as a signal of shame unto those who've forgotten the great.

(*She bends down and lays the wreath at the foot of the Memorial; the* COUPLES *below show signs of uneasiness.*)

GUARDSMAN (*over to the other* COUPLE). Let's leave 'ere, en go into the fresh ire, wha'?

(*The* COUPLES, *with their arms round each other, cross each other, one* COUPLE *to the right, the other to the left, and go slowly out, while the* OLD WOMAN *is singing the verse of the song—)*

OLD WOMAN (*singing softly, with head a little bent as she stands before the Figure*):

Young men sing to the maids in the red beams of the sun;
In the red beams of the sun the maids sing to the young men.
New life's born in the young minds beneath the white gleam of the moon;
But deep in the black earth's lying now a red-plum'd dragoon!

When his hand held a maid's her cheeks blossom'd to red,
Her white breasts grew firm as her cheeks blossom'd to red;
Her emptiness thrill'd to be big with the fruit of his love—
But deep in the black earth's lying now the red-plum'd dragoon!

(*She raises her arms over her head, looking up as she does so.*)

(*Speaking*) O God, of the great promises, give peace and show Thou mercy unto the golden life that's gone!

(*She turns away slowly, and, with dragging feet, comes down the slope, singing softly and bitterly as she goes slowly out.*)

OLD WOMAN (*singing*):

May God in a rage smite the world to its end;
May God in a red rage smite the whole world to its end;
May the white kindness of God change soon to the lightning that kills,
For deep in the black earth's lying now a red-plum'd dragoon!

(*As the* OLD WOMAN *goes out—from the opposite direction the arguing group, consisting of the* MAN IN THE TRILBY, *the* MAN IN THE BOWLER HAT, *the* MAN WITH THE STICK, *and others, re-enter, still arguing—but on another subject, and pass round with the same staccato movements as before, talking as they go, till finally they settle in the centre of the scene.*

MAN IN THE BOWLER HAT, *as he comes in*—)

MAN IN THE BOWLER HAT. 'Course you can feel en' hear when you're unconscious. You're unconscious when you're asleep, but you still have the faculty of feeling en' hearing.

MAN IN THE TRILBY. No, sir, no; all the so-called senses are dormant in a styte of unconsciousness.

MAN WITH THE STICK (*from behind*). Wot abaht en alawm clock agoing off first thing in the mawning?

MAN IN THE TRILBY. You 'ear it only when you become conscious of its striking.

MAN IN THE BOWLER HAT. 'Ow does it wyeken you up, then?

MAN IN THE TRILBY. It doesn't wyeken you up, it can't wyeken you up till you become conscious of its sahnd. You understand thet, surely?

MAN IN THE BOWLER HAT. I understend, but I don't agree. Wot I sye is, while I'm asleep, which is a styte of unconsciousness, I 'ear.

MAN WITH THE STICK. 'Course 'e 'ears!

MAN IN THE TRILBY. The styte of unconsciousness implies a condition unaccompanied by conscious experience. We experience something when we 'ear; 'ow then can we, when we're unconscious, pass into the experience of 'earing?

MAN WITH THE STICK. You're confusing the issue: let's decide first wot is 'earing: now wot do we mean when we say we 'ear?

MAN IN THE TRILBY. The sense of 'earing exists simply as the sense of feeling exists, manifested, for instance, in pleasure or pine, though we know thet pine is non-existent, strictly speaking.

MAN IN THE BOWLER HAT (*scornfully*). Pine non-existent? Oh, don't be silly, man!

MAN WITH THE STICK (*with disgust*). Aw, 'e's a giving us Christian Science now!

MAN IN THE BOWLER HAT. Mean to sye you carn't feel the jeb of a pin or the sting of a wasp?

MAN IN THE TRILBY. You can, if you want to feel them.

MAN WITH THE STICK. Can if you—but no one warnts to feel them. Aw! We're back again at where we sterted.

MAN IN THE BOWLER HAT (*to the* MAN WITH THE STICK). Wite a minute, wite a minute; impatience'll never get at the truth of things. (*To the* MAN IN THE TRILBY) Suppose you cut your finger, wouldn't you feel pine?

MAN IN THE TRILBY. I'm not going to suppose enything of the kind. As mind willed pine into existence, so mind c'n will pine awye again.

MAN WITH THE STICK (*with impatience*). Aw!

MAN IN THE BOWLER HAT (*to the* MAN WITH THE STICK). Wite a minute, wite a minute. (*To the* MAN IN THE TRILBY) You said thet if you cut your finger, you wouldn't feel pine?

MAN IN THE TRILBY. I never said enything of the kind.

MAN WITH THE STICK. Never said—aw! We 'eard you syeing it, pline.

MAN IN THE TRILBY. I've argued in a general wye, en' I won't be refuted by a trivial perticukular, the genesis of which I deny: you carn't cut your finger.

MAN WITH THE STICK (*with consternation*). Carn't cut your—oh, mister, mister, mister!

MAN IN THE BOWLER HAT (*indignantly to the* MAN WITH THE STICK). Wite a minute, wite a minute, carn't you, en' give me a charnce!

(*During this discussion, the group has been joined by a huge, angular, big-headed man, with wild, staring eyes, large, expansive hands, and long, clumsily formed feet.*

He is dressed in a dirty, well-worn yellow burberry, grey flannel trousers a little too short for him, a large-brimmed, old slouch hat, the brim falling down both sides of his head. With his big hands he thrusts the CROWD *aside into a wondering semicircle round himself, and they stand and listen good-humouredly to the rambling things he has to say.*)

MAN IN THE BURBERRY (*with wild excitement*). Listen to me, my good people, listen to me!

(*He opens his mouth in a wide, stupid grin, and stares at those gathered round him with his big, bulging eyes.*)

(*With wild animation*) Why's there different thoughts in every mind, en' different rules in every country? Because the whole world is upside down, my good people. What do I mean when I says the world is upside down? Why, I means that the world is upside down, en' people as have brains'll understand me! Ooooouh!

(*He waves his arms about, jumps a few feet from the ground with a stiff effort, and gives a loud, hilarious, groaning shout.*)

There's some people in this crowd'll understand what I'm saying, en' some people in this crowd'll not understand what I'm saying, because some people in this crowd has brains, en' some people in this crowd is only living in hopes. What do I mean? Why have some people too much to eat, while others has to live on air? Because, good people, the world is upside down!

MAN WITH THE STICK (*shoving his way to the front*). Excuse me, Mr. Speaker, question.

MAN IN THE BURBERRY (*impatiently—facing*

towards the interrupter, and pawing the air as a boxer might do). Wait a minute, wait a minute, wait a minute! Give us a chance to get going. (*Turning the other way*) Am I against sport? Do I object to people amusing theirselves? Did I say so? No, my good people, I love to see people amusing theirselves.

MAN WITH THE STICK (*a little louder than before*). Eh, Mr. Speaker, just a minute: question.

MAN IN THE BURBERRY (*indignantly waving his hands towards the interrupter*). Wait a minute, wait a minute. (*Turning away again*) Now, what do I believe in, good people? (*Solemnly*) I believe in a God who created all things.

MAN WITH THE STICK (*with a gesture of despair*). Aw, he's spoiling everything now!

MAN IN THE BURBERRY (*protestingly to the* CROWD). How can I be expected to solve things if I'm constantly interrupted? (*Resuming his oratorical manner.*) No, good people, there's a few things in the world we can't understand. We has to cultivate the earth if we want to get the things she has to give. Now, what do I mean? Steady! I want thinkers! We has to do things if we wants things done. Shoulder to the wheel, shove, en' get things going: a man's job, en' after to amuse hisself. En' what is man? Steady! Why man is man, en' more than man, en' people with brains'll understand what I means!

MAN WITH THE STICK (*with resolution*). Eh, there, Mr. Speaker, abaht this question of wot man is en' 'ow 'e originyted, let's get things into definite shipe.

(*He taps the* MAN IN THE BURBERRY *on the back with his stick.*)

Did 'e escipe from the pithecanthropus stite, or did 'e come dahn direct from the Neanderthal—

(*The* MAN IN THE BURBERRY, *frightened at this opposition, begins to slink away out of the* CROWD.)

(*Calling out*) Eh, don't go awye, don't run off, till we settle this question once f'r all.

(*The* MAN IN THE BURBERRY *breaks through the* CROWD, *makes for the centre path, crosses the slope and goes out.*

MAN WITH THE STICK (*following and calling after him*). It's some sleep en' a lot of nourishment you warn't, en' not knowledge!

(*The members of the* CROWD *disperse; some following the* MAN WITH THE STICK, *who has followed the* MAN IN THE BURBERRY; *some round the path by the lake; some to the right and some to the left.*

After a moment or two, the YOUNG WHORE *enters with the* DREAMER. *She is leaning heavily on his arm. Her breathing is quick; her face is very pale, and in her eyes is a fixed look of fear. The lie of her clothing shows that she has dressed hastily. She is dressed as before, in black, slashed with crimson.*

The DREAMER *wears a vivid orange scarf thrown carelessly round his neck and shoulders. He leads the* YOUNG WHORE *to a bench opposite to that on which the* EVANGELISTS are sitting.)

YOUNG WHORE (*tremulously*). I'm bad, I'm in a bad way; oh, please go and find the Bishop for me.

DREAMER (*encouragingly*). Don't be afraid, dear; it's only over-excitement, created with a fear that's foolish.

YOUNG WHORE (*mechanically stroking her dress into order*). Everything seems to be on me every way and any way. (*With a wan smile*) You hurried me into them, Dreamer, as quick as you hurried me out of them. . . . Things are jumping and twisting before my eyes. . . . (*Frightened*) Get the Bishop, go and get the Bishop!

DREAMER. Can't you get comfort and courage from me?

YOUNG WHORE (*tonelessly*). I want the Bishop. He's been following me about for days, and I know I need him now. Go up to the slope and, if you see him, at least tell me, that I may call him to me.

(*After a moment's hesitation—*

The DREAMER *goes slowly up to the slope and stands there looking about him.*

The YOUNG WHORE *sits motionless, staring out in front of her.*

The YOUNG MAN IN PLUS-FOURS *comes in, stops and looks at her, but she takes no notice. He goes over and strokes her knee, but she does not move. He looks at her wonderingly, goes a few paces from her, turns and looks at her again, then goes out.*

The GARDENER *comes up the path leading from the lake. He is lilting softly to himself.*)

GARDENER (*lilting*):

Since Adam first ventur'd to fall,
And Eve took a hand in th' venturesome game,
Life's banner's turn'd into a shawl—

(*He stops and stares at the* YOUNG WHORE.)

Jannice! Is that you, Jannice? (*He goes closer to her.*) What's wrong? (*He puts his hand on her shoulder.*) Aren't you going to say a kind word for old times' sake? No? Oh, well, we can do without it.

(*He goes up path leading to slope, lilting to himself.*)

Let the pray'r-busy bishop akneel in his stall,
Drone deep in a measur'd, liturgical drawl—
Th' pleasures of love are all sweeten'd with gall:
I and the crowd don't believe it at all—
Desire for a woman's both worship and play;
And so I'll dance with a girl in a hall,
At the end, at the end, at the ending of day!

(*The* DREAMER *strolls about on the slope, sometimes passing from view to the right, sometimes to the left. Just now he is unseen as the* BISHOP'S SISTER *appears there, looking anxiously round her. She looks snug and warm in a heavy coat, with a fur collar circling her neck. As she appears above, the* OLD WOMAN *comes below. She is greatly bent, and walks with slow and dragging feet. She shivers as she peers about, and catches sight of the* YOUNG WHORE *sitting on the bench. She staggers over to her.*)

OLD WOMAN. For God's sake tell me if you've seen the Bishop anywhere? I am in need, and he must help.

(*As the* YOUNG WHORE *does not answer, she looks closer.*)

It's you, is it? So here you are, pale, very pale, en' looking as if you were settling down for death. Remember now, the way you treated your poor mother. No fancy plumes in front of you now—only the last things staring you straight in the face!

YOUNG WHORE (*doggedly—with a vicious look at the* OLD WOMAN). Anyhow, if I go, I'll go game, and die dancing.

OLD WOMAN (*venomously*). Looks as if it was me would be dancing over your grave, my merry lady.

(*The* YOUNG WHORE *gets to her feet and walks unsteadily away from the* OLD WOMAN, *till she is met by the* BISHOP'S SISTER *who has come down from the slope. The* YOUNG WHORE *retreats a few steps so that she is between them both, where she stands shivering.*)

BISHOP'S SISTER (*angrily to the* YOUNG WHORE). I've come across you, have I? Waiting for the Bishop's help and pity, are you? Be off out of the Park and hide yourself, you shameless thing, or I'll send the Police down on you!

OLD WOMAN (*to the* BISHOP'S SISTER). En' who may you be, mademoiselle?

BISHOP'S SISTER. I'm the Bishop's Sister.

OLD WOMAN (*bowing almost to the ground—mockingly*). Salaam, mem pukka memsahib, salaam, en' pardon her, en' pardon me, en' pardon us all for getting in the way of thy greatness; en' grant us grace to have faith in thy dignity en' importance, per benedicite pax hugger muggery ora pro puggery rigmarolum!

BISHOP'S SISTER (*to* YOUNG WHORE). Such as you ought to be stretched out naked on the ground for every decent woman to trample the life out of you!

OLD WOMAN (*mutteringly*). We wouldn't be trampled to death, sister, we wouldn't be trampled to death.

BISHOP'S SISTER (*violently*). Sympathy for such as you would be a sin. The helping hand of pity must be turned into the punishing hand of bronze.

OLD WOMAN (*remonstratively*). Oh, sister, sister.

BISHOP'S SISTER (*furiously*). How dare you call me sister!

OLD WOMAN (*reflectively*). How savage we can be when God has been unkind and made us plain, and man can find no vision in our looks!

(*During the last few phrases the* TWO PLACARDED EVANGELISTS *have appeared on the slope above from the left, and the* TWO CHAIR ATTENDANTS *from the right. They are bent, and move on tottering legs. They meet in the centre and come down the centre path two by two. They then part, the* TWO EVANGELISTS *going to the right, and the* TWO CHAIR ATTENDANTS *going to the left. A stillness falls on the scene, broken only by the sharp calls of the gulls. The three women look at the men silently. In the distance can then be heard the drum-tap, slow and doleful, and the murmur of the chant of the* DOWN-AND-OUTS. *The* OLD WOMAN *and the* YOUNG WHORE *stiffen and listen to the murmuring chant.)*

OLD WOMAN, YOUNG WHORE *(together)*. The chant and the drum-beat of the Down-and-Outs!

TWO CHAIR ATTENDANTS, TWO EVANGELISTS *(together)*. We fled from before them till all our strength was gone.

(The BISHOP *appears on the slope above. He stands so that the light from the lamp falls on him, a sad and dignified figure in his cassock with its crimson buttons,*

and the heavy cross lying upon his breast. He leans rather heavily on his staff, stretches out his arm, extends two of his fingers over the heads of those below, and blesses them in sad and low tones, slightly intoning the words.)

BISHOP. Benedicti vos a Domino, qui fecit coelum et terram.

(*The* YOUNG WHORE *rushes over to the centre, falls on her knees, and raises her hands up towards the* BISHOP.)

YOUNG WHORE (*imploringly*). Bless me, even me, oh my father!

(*With a convulsive shiver and a quivering lip, the* BISHOP *stretches out his arm towards the* YOUNG WHORE, *extends two fingers to bless her, but his arm falls slowly to his side and he remains silent.*)

(*Imploringly*) Bless me, even me, also, oh my father!

(*The* BISHOP *comes down a few steps, again stretches out his arm and extends two fingers to bless her, but his arm slowly falls to his side, and he remains silent.*

The DREAMER *appears on the slope, and stands in the light where the* BISHOP *stood, looking at those below him. The*

BISHOP *comes down farther, passes the* YOUNG WHORE, *who is almost lying on the ground, and stands in the centre, with half of the group on his left, and the other half to his right.*)

BISHOP'S SISTER (*in low and bitter tones*). Woe to her that is filthy, that obeyed not the voice, and received not correction.

(*The drum-tap of the* DOWN-AND-OUTS *is heard a little nearer, and the words of the chant take shape, but the sound is still in the distance, and is heard faintly, but clearly.*)

DOWN-AND-OUTS (*chanting in the distance*):

We challenge life no more with our dead faith, or our dead hope;
We carry furled the flags of our dead hope and our dead faith;
Day sings no song, neither is there room for rest beside night in her sleeping:
Life has left us but a sigh for a song, and a deep sigh for a drum-beat!

YOUNG WHORE (*despairingly*). They are coming for me, they are coming for me at last!

TWO EVANGELISTS, OLD WOMAN, TWO ATTENDANTS (*together*):

Turn our feet away, O Lord, from the way of them in whose eyes is no brightness;

Whose long dead hearts singeth no old nor any
new song.

1ST CHAIR ATTENDANT. Envy, hatred, and malice are in our hearts, and we covet the goods of our neighbour.

2ND CHAIR ATTENDANT. Yea, Lord; yet we stand no worse than most men are.

1ST EVANGELIST. We have labour'd to set Thee fair and square before them forgetful of Thy greatness; and before all who are senseless of their need of Thee.

BISHOP. We beseech Thee to hear them, good Lord.

DREAMER. Let them sink into the grave, O Lord; and never let their like appear upon the face of the earth again.

1ST CHAIR ATTENDANT. Under the hedge, or snug in the tuck'd up bed, with reckless women, we have laughed our way in and out to sin.

2ND CHAIR ATTENDANT. Yea, Lord, all this have we done; yet stand we now, no worse than most men are.

1ST EVANGELIST. We have danced no dance, neither have we searched for the hidden beauty of women; we have sung no songs, nor have we made merry in our hearts.

2ND EVANGELIST. We have honour'd pain; bound up joy with sighing; and multiplied sorrows that men might know Thy mercy and Thy loving kindness.

BISHOP. We beseech Thee to hear them, good Lord.

DREAMER. Let them sink into the grave, O Lord; and never let their like appear upon the face of the earth again.

1ST CHAIR ATTENDANT. We have failed to bother much about Thy commandments, and have laid hands on all things that came our way without thanking Thee.

2ND CHAIR ATTENDANT. Yea, Lord, all this have we done; yet stand we now, no worse than all men are.

1ST EVANGELIST. Stricken, we struck not back; we blessed them that cursed us; and prayed for them that mocked at our concern for the souls of men.

BISHOP. Hear their prayer, O Lord, and let their cry come unto Thee.

DREAMER. Let brambles, O Lord, grow thick where they are buried deep; let the fox and the vixen guard their cubs in the midst of the brambles; and let children sing and laugh and play where they have moaned in their misery!

(*The* DOWN-AND-OUTS *are now very near, and their chant is heard as if they were present. The first part of the chant is sung before they appear on the slope above.)*

DOWN-AND-OUTS (*chanting*):

Life has pass'd by us to the loud roll of her drum,
With her waving flags of yellow and green held high,
All starr'd with the golden, flaming names of her most mighty children.

Oh, where shall we go when the day calls?
Oh, where shall we sleep when the night falls?
We've but a sigh for a song, and a deep sigh for a drum-beat!

(*They have entered on the slope above, moving at a snail's pace, all bent, haggard, and utterly miserable. The* YOUNG WHORE *rises slowly and painfully to her feet as they chant the second part of their miserere.)*

We challenge life no more, no more, with our dead faith and our dead hope;
We carry furled the fainting flags of a dead hope and a dead faith.
Day sings no song, neither is there room for rest beside night in her sleeping:
We've but a sigh for a song, and a deep sigh for a drum-beat.

(*The* DREAMER *takes the orange scarf from*

about his neck, and winds it round his waist like a sash. The YOUNG WHORE *goes unsteadily a little nearer to the* BISHOP.)

YOUNG WHORE (*appealingly to the* BISHOP). Let me not mingle my last moments with this marching misery!

BISHOP (*slowly and with decision*). With them, daughter, is safety and penance, and penance will bring you peace.

(*The* YOUNG WHORE *turns away from the* BISHOP, *and goes up the centre towards the* DOWN-AND-OUTS, *who come down as if to meet her; but they halt when they find that the* DREAMER *bars their way down. The* YOUNG WHORE *goes on with her head bent till she finds herself in the arms of the* DREAMER. *She struggles faintly to free herself, but he holds her tight.*)

BISHOP (*to the* YOUNG WHORE, *slowly and with decision*). You must go where they go, and their sighing shall be your song. You must mingle your last hour with the dust that marching life has left behind her.

DOWN-AND-OUTS (*chanting*):

You must be merry no more; you must walk in the midst of the mournful;

Who've but a sigh for a song, and a deep sigh for a drum-beat.

TWO EVANGELISTS, BISHOP'S SISTER, CHAIR ATTENDANTS, OLD WOMAN (*together*):

She who was merry shall now walk in the midst of the mournful,
Who've but a sigh for a song, and a deep sigh for a drum-beat!

(*The* YOUNG WHORE *has stiffened with resentment as she listens and now stands facing the* DREAMER, *looking longingly at him for encouragement.*)

DREAMER (*to the* YOUNG WHORE). Turn your back swift on the poor, purple-button'd deadman, whose name is absent from the book of life. Offer not as incense to God the dust of your sighing, but dance to His glory, and come before His presence with a song!

YOUNG WHORE (*with reckless defiance*). I'll go the last few steps of the way rejoicing; I'll go, go game, and I'll die dancing!

DREAMER (*exultantly*). Sing them silent, dance them still, and laugh them into an open shame!

(*Faintly, as if the tune was heard only in the minds of the* DREAMER *and the* YOUNG WHORE, *the notes of a dance tune are heard, coming from the subdued playing of a flute and other instruments. The* YOUNG WHORE *and the* DREAMER *dance to the melody, she a little unsteadily. They dance for about a minute, then the movements of the* YOUNG WHORE *become a little uncertain; she staggers, recovers herself, dances again, but with faltering steps. The music of the dance becomes fainter.*)

YOUNG WHORE (*frightened*). Dreamer, Dreamer, I'm fainting—I think I'm going to die.

DREAMER (*fiercely*). Sing them silent; dance them still; laugh them into an open shame!

DOWN-AND-OUTS (*chanting and coming down a little by the centre*):

She must be merry no more; she must be set in the midst of the mournful,
Who've but a sigh for a song, and a deep sigh for a drum-beat.

DREAMER (*fiercely, with his face close to the* YOUNG WHORE'S). Sing them silent; dance them still; laugh them into an open shame!

BISHOP (*sinking down on his knees, and intoning the words*). O Lord, most mighty, O holy and most merciful Saviour, deliver not this poor, dolorous soul into the pains of eternal death!

(*The* DREAMER *and the* YOUNG WHORE

again dance to the music of a flute and other instruments. The tune is now slow and mournful, and the DREAMER *is almost carrying the* YOUNG WHORE *in his arms. They dance in this way for a few moments, then the head of the* YOUNG WHORE *falls limp, and the* DREAMER *lifts her in his arms, carries her to the foot of the slope, and lays her gently on the ground.*)

YOUNG WHORE (*almost in a whisper*). I die, Dreamer, I die, and my soul is heavy with a great fear.

DREAMER (*standing over her, gently*). Fear nothing; God will find room for one scarlet blossom among His thousand white lilies.

(*The* BISHOP *rises from his knees and goes over to where she is lying. He kneels again, and takes one of her hands in his.*)

YOUNG WHORE (*staring at the* BISHOP). Guide the hand you hold into making the sign of the cross, that I may whisper my trust in the golden mercy of God.

(*The* BISHOP *guides her hand as she makes the sign of the cross. She lies still and silent. The* DOWN-AND-OUTS *come down centre, chanting. They spread out, enveloping, first, the* TWO EVAN-

GELISTS, *next*, *the* OLD WOMAN, *and finally*, the TWO CHAIR ATTENDANTS.)

DOWN-AND-OUTS (*chanting*):

We challenge life no more, no more, with our dead faith, or our dead hope;
We carry furl'd the fainting flags of a dead hope and a dead faith.
Day sings no song, neither is there room for rest beside night in her sleeping:
We've but a sigh for a song, and a deep sigh for a drum-beat!

DREAMER:

Way for the strong and the swift and the fearless:
Life that is stirr'd with the fear of its life, let it die;
Let it sink down, let it die, and pass from our vision forever.
Sorrow and pain we shall have, and struggle unending:
We shall weave courage with pain, and fight through the struggle unending.
Way for the strong and the swift and the fearless:
Life that is weak with the terror of life let it die;
Let it sink down, let it die, and pass from our vision forever!

(*The* EVANGELISTS, *the* CHAIR ATTEND-

ANTS, *and the* OLD WOMAN *are hidden in the midst of the* DOWN-AND-OUTS *who march slowly out chanting their miserere.*)

OLD WOMAN (*calling shrilly, appealingly, and despairingly from among the* DOWN-AND-OUTS *as they go out*). Gilbert!

(*The* DOWN-AND-OUTS *pass out. The* BISHOP *is kneeling beside the* YOUNG WHORE. *The* DREAMER *has gone up the centre path, and is standing on the slope looking down. The* BISHOP'S SISTER *stands to the left, with her eyes fixed on the kneeling* BISHOP.)

BISHOP'S SISTER (*tensely to the* BISHOP). Why did that old woman shrill out the name of Gilbert? (*He is silent.*) Do you hear me? Why did that old woman shrill out the name of Gilbert?

BISHOP (*in a low and terrible voice, without turning his head*). Go home, go home, for Christ's sake, woman, and ask God's mercy on us all!

(*The* BISHOP'S SISTER *looks at the kneeling figure for a moment, then, turning, without another word, she goes slowly out.*

The DREAMER *comes down the slope to-*

wards the BISHOP, *and stops when he is half-way down.)*

DREAMER (*looking towards the* BISHOP *and the figure of the* YOUNG WHORE). Hail and farewell, sweetheart; forever and forever, hail and farewell!

BISHOP (*in low and grief-stricken tones*). She died making the sign of the cross, she died making the sign of the cross!

(*The* DREAMER *gazes for a moment at the* YOUNG WHORE, *then turns and begins to go slowly out. The music, sounding slow and soft, of the song he sang to her is heard; in the middle of the melody the gates begin to close slowly, coming together on the last few notes of the tune.*)

MUSIC TO THE PLAY

MUSIC TO THE PLAY

Composed and adapted by HERBERT HUGHES

SPRING CHORUS

Founded on "Haste to the Wedding"

SCENE I

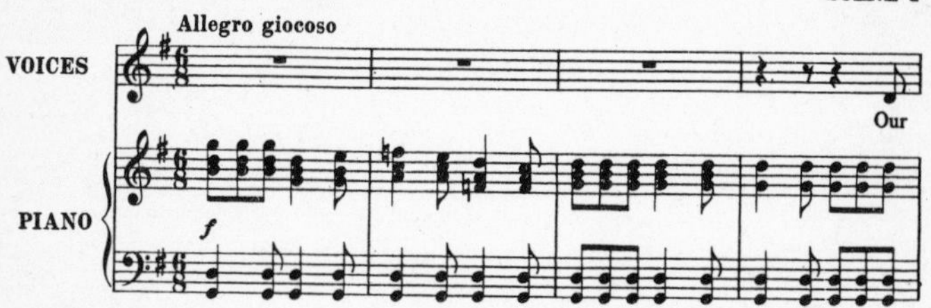

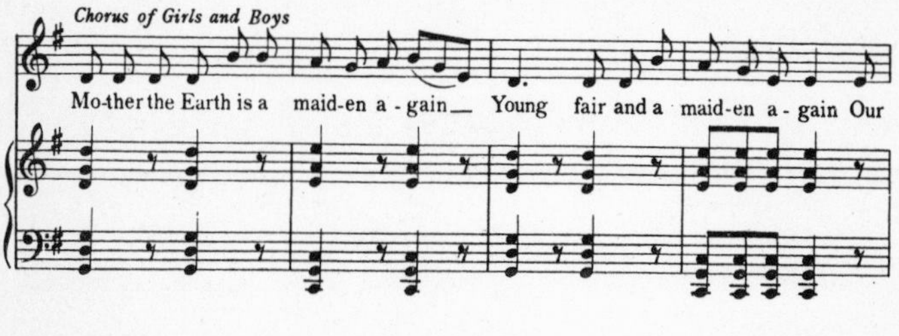

The music is scored for a chamber orchestra consisting of flute (interchangeable with piccolo) two violins, viola, cello, double-bass, vibraphone and percussion.

The percussion consists of side-drum, cymbals, triangle and bass-drum, sparingly used; these, and the vibraphone, should be played by one person

Her thoughts are a dance as she
seeks out her bride - groom the sun through the
love - ly con-fus - ion of sing-ing of birds and of blos-som and bud.

She feels the touch of his hand on her hair, on her cheeks, in the
Flute
mf
bud - ding of trees
She feels the kiss of his love on her
cresc.
ff Crowd joins in
mouth, on her breast as she dan - ces a - long
Through the
cresc.
ff

love-ly con-fus - ion of sing-ing of birds, and of blos-som and bud Her
f
thoughts are a dance as she seeks out her bride - groom the
f
sun through the love-ly con-fus - ion of sing-ing of birds and of
blos-som and bud.

Chorus only
mf
She hears the fierce-ly-sung song of the birds bu-sy
Flute
mf
build-ing new homes in the hedge
She hears a chal-lenge to
2
life and to death as she dan - ces a-long
cresc.
cresc.

Crowd joins in
Through — the lovely confusion of singing of birds and of
blossom and bud Her thoughts are a dance as she
seeks out her bridegroom the sun Through the lovely confusion of
singing of birds and of blossom and bud

ff All
Our Mo-ther the Earth is a maid-en a-gain
Young, fair and a maid-en a-gain. Our Mo-ther the Earth is a
maid-en a-gain She's young and is fair and a
maid-en a-gain

I'M NOT THINKING OF BLOSSOMS AT ALL

SCENE I

Then I'll dance with a girl in a hall When the
Then I'll dance with a girl in a hall When the
sink-ing sun says it's the end of the day
sink-ing sun says it's the end of the day
All sweet-scent-ed blos-soms long thoughts can re-call
Words of the gos-pel on deaf-en'd ear fall And

Fair in their bloom and sweet still in their fall
Joy of the saints is a joy that is small To the
Bloom a-gain and with pride hid-den un-der a shawl
joy and the joys nest - ling un-der a shawl
ritard.
ritard.
ritard.
a tempo
I'm not think-ing of blos-soms at all Let them
I'm not think-ing of heav-en at all It's a
a tempo
a tempo

flour-ish and die in the old fash-ioned way
dy-ing out star a long dis-tance a-way
For I'll dance with a girl in a hall At the end, at the end at the ending of
For I'll dance with a girl in a hall At the end, at the end at the ending of
day.
day.

The Crowd Sings. (The Young Whore enters hurriedly, but without spoiling the ordered movements of the singers and mixes with the crowd)
Since poor Ad-am first ven-tur'd to fall. And
Eve took a hand in the ven-ture-some game
Life's banners turn'd in-to a
shawl Deep - fring'd with de-sire and spear-point-ed with flame
Flute
Let the pray'r-bu-sy bis-hop a-kneel in his stall Drone

deep in a meas-ur'd li-tur-gi-cal drawl That the
plea - sures of poor are all sweet-en'd with gall.
I and the crowd don't be-lieve it at all De -
-sire for a wom-an's both wor-ship and play And
cresc.
cresc.
ff
Flute
dim.
f

dim.
so I'll dance with a girl in a hall at the end, at the end, at the
dim.
pp
end - ing of day.
pp
Vibraphone
Strings
Vibraphone

SUMMER CHORUS

SCENE II

Stor - ing the best of your life in a draw'r of your desk at the of - fice
Rack - ing your life for the hope of a co - sy cor - ner in heav-en
Till the wide ear of the wide world is deaf - en'd with wis-dom
Bel-low good-bye to the beg-gar-in' lot 'n come
out To bow down the head 'n bend down the knee to the bee 'n the bird 'n the
blossom Bann - 'ring the breast of the earth with a won -
8va bassa

ten.
-der-ful beau-ty
Ye who have prison'd your life in the black and the gau-dy red gown of the law-courts Or
think that your breast is the glit-ter-ing sky when it's wear-ing the star of an or-der
Ye who ply hammer an' saw or toil at a lathe in a work-shop
Bellow good

-bye to the beg-gar-in' lot 'n come out to
8
8va bassa.
bow down the head 'n bend down the knee to the bee to the bird 'n the
blos-som Bann - 'ring the breast of the earth with a
3
3
won - der-ful beau-ty
Picc.

JANNICE

Founded on an Irish tune

SCENE II

down from the heights of a pil - low
Tossed by
a soft breeze in the spring The blooms of an apple tree bil - low; And her
breasts are as love-ly to me Look-ing down from the heights of a pil -
-low Look - ing down from the heights of a pil - low

Gay white ap-ple blossoms her breast, Her legs golden branches of
molto legato
wil - low; I'd en - joy for a year and a day Look - ing
down from the heights of a pil - low Look - ing
down from the heights of a pil - low.

SING AND DANCE!

AIR: "Little Brown Jug" *by R. A. Eastburn* **SCENE III**

Chair Attendants join in
joy in-stead, For we will be a long time dead, Sling aht woe, 'ug joy in-stead, For
Fine
we will be a long time dead.
SALVATIONISTS' HYMN
SCENE III
YOUNG OFFICER
Be-fore Thy cross, O Lord, we bow, And claim Thy faith-ful prom-ise
Show, Lord the calm of Cal-va-ry To fright-en'd souls that cry to
now; These sin-ned souls make white as snow That they Thy peace may know.
Thee; Cag'd fast in doubt, half-mad with fear, Oh bring Thy par-don near.
Salvationists join in
These sin-ned souls make white as snow That they Thy peace may know.
Cag'd fast in doubt, half-mad with fear, Oh, bring Thy par-don near!

THE RED PLUMED DRAGOON

Founded on an Irish Tune

SCENE IV

life's born in the young maids be - neath the white_ gleam of the moon But
empti - ness thrill'd to be big_with the fruit of his love But

deep in the black earth's ly - ing now a red plum'd dra - goon.
deep in the black earth's ly - ing now the red plum'd dra - goon.
cresc.

OLD WOMAN (speaking) "O God of the great promises, give peace
and show Thou mercy unto the golden life that's gone"
When his
May
f
dim.

God in a rage smite the world to its end, May
God in a red rage smite the whole world to its
end; May the white kind-ness of God change
soon to the light-ning that kills For
f
dim.
dim.

deep in the black earth's ly-ing now
add B.D.
p
p
— a red plum'd dra-
dim.
dim.
pp
-goon.
pp senza rall.

SONG OF THE DOWN AND OUTS*

* Fragments of this music are heard in each of the preceding scenes

where shall we go when the night falls? We've but a sigh ___ for a song and a
-side ___ night in her sleep - ing; For we've but a sigh ___ for a song and a
dim.
mf
deep ___ sigh for a drum - beat ___
deep ___ sigh for a drum - beat ___
The Young Whore turns away from the Bishop, and goes up the centre towards the Down and Outs, who come down as if to meet her, but they halt when they find that the Dreamer bars their way down. She goes on with her head bent till she finds herself in the arms of the Dreamer. She struggles faintly to free herself, but he holds her tight.
BISHOP (to the Young Whore): "You must go where they go, and their sighing shall be your song. You must mingle your last hour with the dust that marching life has left behind her"
(DOWN & OUTS) She must be mer-ry no more; she must walk in the midst of the mourn - ful
(TWO EVANGELISTS etc) She who was mer - ry shall now walk in the midst of the mourn - ful
p
Who've but a sigh ___ for a song and a deep ___ sigh for a drum - beat
Who've but a sigh ___ for a song and a deep ___ sigh for a drum - beat
pp
dim.
ppp

JANNICE'S DANCE

SCENE IV

WAY FOR THE STRONG!

SCENE IV